Ordinarily Extraordinary

N. Raghuraman

Foreward

Subhash Chandra

Ocean Paperbacks

A Division of Ocean Books Pvt. Ltd.

ISO 9001:2008 Publishers

Published by
Ocean Paperbacks
A Division of Ocean Books Pvt. Ltd.
4/19 Asaf Ali Road,
New Delhi-110 002 (INDIA)
Phs.: 011-23289555 • 23289777
E-mail: info@oceanbooks.in

ISBN 978-81-8430-253-0
Ordinarily Extraordinary
by N. Raghuraman

Edition
2016

Price
₹ 175.00 (Rs. One Hundred Seventy Five only)

Printed at
Narula Printers, Delhi

~~~~~~~~~~~~~~~~~~~~~~~~~~~~~~~~~~~

In memory of

my loving parents

Jayalakshmi & V.N. Rajan

~~~~~~~~~~~~~~~~~~~~~~~~~~~~~~~~~~~

Acknowledgement

I owe a deep sense of gratitude all those who have been a source of inspiration and encouragement in bringing out this book. I sincerely thank Mr. Subhash Chandra, Chairman, Zee Group for writing an appropriate forward for this book.

I am extremely thankful to DB Group chairman, Mr. Ramesh Chandra Agarwal, Managing Director, Mr Sudhir Agarwal and Directors Girish Agarwal and Pawan Agarwal.

I am thankful to my wife Prema and daughter Nishevita who ungrudgingly tolerated my persistent absence from their lives. They are my inspiration, my life and my every breath.

Am beholden to my parents who always believed that, good things happening around must be identified and appreciated.

Foreword

It is disturbing to see how basic human values are fast crumbling around us. Everything is so frothy, so ephemeral. Where have emotions like love, compassion and respect for elders vanished? Well, we can't put all the blame squarely on those who have strayed. Maybe somewhere, we, who are the more mature and responsible in the society, have failed in our duty as citizens in providing Young India, as indeed all others, a direction. Young India, maybe at times, even a wee-bit disappointing. Young India is impatient, a bit too impatient, not quite attuned to the adage of sustained efforts and the consequent rewards.

It's here that I find Mr N Raghuraman's book, is enterprising. Drawing on his long-standing experience as a journalist and motivational speaker, he is secure in the knowledge that mere high-end didacticism in an elaborately-adorned language does not necessarily inspire. What makes a desired difference is simplicity of thoughts strung together by simple incidents culled out from life's vicissitudes and provoking the reader to stop a while to consider. These crisp essays on various themes, ranging from friendship, compassion, reverence for elders, steeled resolve as a conduit to achievement and many more such themes is, in short, a simple book with real-life asides. The intention: Reminding people of those quintessential values of life which they have so conveniently forgotten. On reading, the book comes through as an earnest effort to cajole, cuddle and inspire - all done unobtrusively - those who may have slipped and also those who haven't but need that little nudge to hitch their wagon to a star. The book gently asks you to think sharp with determination, but with a heart, as that is what can set you going on the route to success.

I believe that if you want to do something dearly, you won't care how successful you are. Your duty as a responsible citizen is what will drive you to do it with your hard-earned expertise. The acknowledgement of the effort, I believe, is the reward of the enterprise.

I wish Raghuraman all luck with his book and hope his efforts find due acknowledgement as that would be his reward.

—Subhash Chandra
Chairman, Zee Group

Contents

SECTION-II

SECTION-III

SECTION-V

SECTION-I

Love Makes The World Go Round

1

Sow Courtesy, Reap Love

Case I: 1955. Allahabad University. Gayatri, then an MSc student, recalls an incident with fondness even today. The science department was quite close to the English department. She remembers this Professor of the English department as well-mannered to a fault, dapper and endowed with a distinctive aura, almost reel-like, driving his car with one hand on the wheel and the other negotiating a cigarette.

His innate charm mesmerized the students. His gentle nod each time he met anyone, his genteel smile, his courteous gesture of holding the door open to let the girls in first were attributes that endeared him to all, irrespective of the departments. Not courtesy alone, his erudition was unparalleled. Here was a Professor with equal proficiency in both English and Hindi literatures, a member of the rare breed, who, as a Professor of English, could pen Hindi poetry.

Today, an octogenarian, Gayatri Pachodi, a retired Professor of mathematics, lives in Jabalpur in Madhya Pradesh. And the Professor? You might ask. Well, he was none other than the great scholar-poet, Harivansh Rai

Bachchan of Madhushala fame and father of Bollywood superstar, Amitabh Bachchan.

Case II: 1998. A small lane called Juhu Church Road in Mumbai near the famous Juhu beach. It is within a three-minute walking distance from Amitabh Bachchan's house 'Pratiksha'. Almost at the middle of Juhu Church Road is this old housing complex called Chand Society. A large limousine entering this building every second day is something few haven't noticed. So, what's the big deal, you might ask. Nothing, except that a swanky car is not common in a building inhabited mostly by the middle-class. The four-storeyed building has no lift and is poorly maintained with paint wearing off at various places.

The limousine is almost always driven by a gentleman with a goatee in a spiffy outfit. Upon parking, he disembarks, moves to the other side of the car and opens the door for the occupant who is a lady, wishes her good night and quietly drives back home.

I think I gave him away with the mention of the goatee. Yes, that's Amitabh Bachchan driving his personal secretary of long standing, Rosy Singh, home at Chand Society. Rosy stood by his side when the superstar was eclipsed by the debacle of ABCL, his dream company during the late 1990s. Tiding over the rough patch, Amitabh soon reached out for the skies again. But the actor known for his civility and urbanness, to this day remains grateful to Rosy, who still works for him.

"Courtesy is a silver lining around the dark clouds of civilization. It is the best part of refinement and, in many ways, an art of heroic beauty in the vast gallery of man's cruelty and baseness," said American editor and author, Bryant H. McGill. Impregnated with pomposity and hubris, the modern age has indeed become 'cruel and base'. In such times, Harivansh Rai and Amitabh Bachchan show how he who sows courtesy reaps friendship and how he who plants kindness gathers love. It's not hard to seek. Inculcate courtesy and see the difference.

❐

2

Assume Nothing. Better Ask

I fell in love with Ruksana at first sight. Ensconced in a hotel amid the huge virgin forests in a place called Khaketi in eastern Georgia on a recent trip, the 10-month-old doggie from Turkey was a loveable plump bundle of fur, who was fun to play with and both my friends at the same hotel, Anil Dharkar, veteran journalist and TV cookery serial *Turban Tadka*—"Food Food Channel" anchor and Chef, Harpal Singh Sokhi, agreed. I was playing with the dog one morning, when this gentleman from India, a guest at the hotel, romped down the stairs, threw me a quizzical look and asked me the dog's name.

"Ruksana," I said. "Ah," he said with a know-all air, as if we were novices on canine nomenclature, "the name suggests it's definitely from Madhya Pradesh." I suggested he asked the owner of the dog, the hotel manager, who was a Georgian and had a Turkish wife. When the owner too said the name was Ruksana, the man did a volte-face and said with the same air of apparent erudition, "Well, yes, as I suspected, the name sounds more Iraqi than Georgian." It was then the owner corrected him. "No Sir, the dog is from Turkey and was a gift from my wife's sister." His know-all veneer shattered, the man quietly slipped away.

"Don't make assumptions," said Mexican author, Miguel Angel Ruiz. "Find the courage to ask questions and to express what you really want. Communicate with others to avoid misunderstandings." The man at the hotel was a perfect example of how the mind processes assumptions faster and does not allow information to flow in first and then process the whole available data with the help of your intelligence. Assumptions create a false notion of omniscience, which can lead to embarrassment. The man-made two assumptions. First, when an Indian, that's I, told him the dog's name, he assumed it to be of an Indian breed, but when a Georgian said the same name, he assumed it to be of Iraqi descent. The truth only left him red-faced.

I have known people who told me, "I know what you are thinking," leaving me dumbstruck. If you think you know what's going on inside someone else's head, think again. It is a great self-defence mechanism, but no substitute for actual communication. In fact, it can ruin a relationship. Remember: The best way to know what's going on in someone else's mind is also the riskiest. So, think smart. The smartest solution is: Ask the person.

❐

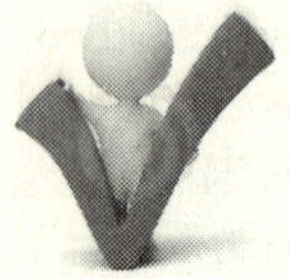

3

Have the Will to Keep Trying

It was only a few days ago that filmmaker Chetan Anand had met Prime Minister Jawaharlal Nehru's personal secretary, O.P. Mathai aboard a flight and the two had discussed meeting the PM. The year was 1963 and the dust had yet to settle on the 1962 Sino-India War. Anand always wanted to make a war film, but the wherewithal needed for its making was daunting. A proper war movie was yet to hit the Indian screen and the producers whom Anand approached were skeptical about its success. But he never gave up. Anand knew in his heart of hearts that his D-day would come, sometime soon.

That's when this chance meeting with Mathai happened, fortuitously, aboard a flight. "Aren't you people tired of making fluffy, chocolaty love stories with mushy songs and running around trees? Your film *Neecha Nagar* was a delight. It was topical. We have just had a humiliating loss of face at the hands of the Chinese. Why don't you make a war film on that?" asked Mathai. "Always wanted to, but never found the support. Platoon, guns, locales, army cooperation..." replied Anand. "*Hmm...*" Mathai was lost in thought for a moment. "Let's meet the PM," he said. "I am told he loves your films. Maybe, he can help."

The meeting happened the following week and Nehru, in all his graceful self, called Minister of Defence, Krishna

Menon and asked him to help out Anand. When Anand left for Jammu the next day, he did not have a script. It was readied in 30 minutes flat aboard the flight on way to Jammu. Anand had always dreamt of making his action sequences big, very big, even in monochrome. It was a tough call. The cast and crew had a harrowing time in the snow-covered environs. Indian cinematography was going through what it had never captured on camera before. Anand knew he had to make it.

Haqeeqat, released in 1964, the first full-fledged war film in India, made history. Cinematography by Sadanand, art direction by M.S. Sathyu, music by Madan Mohan—everything was tuned to perfection. Anand's perseverance bore fruits. *Haqeeqat* remains one of his best films.

Achieving one's goal, the one motto we call success, can't be easily had. There is no short route to success, just as there is no guarantee to getting it. However, one needs to try. Even if you try, there is no guarantee of success, but if you don't, failure is guaranteed. As George Edward Woodberry said, "Defeat is not the worst of failures. Not to have tried is the true failure."

So, time to think smart. Take your pick: Try to succeed. Or don't, to ensure failure. Period.

❐

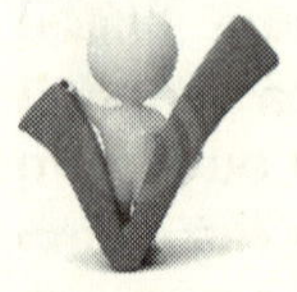

4

Remember and You will be Remembered

Who was this man, I wondered. It was rather unusual for Pixie, my pet dog, to nudge and cuddle up to a stranger.

Morning walks have been second nature since my youth, and summer of 2012 had been hot, hotter than many sweltering summers Mumbai had seen in the past. So, I usually made it an hour earlier than my normal routine before the crack of dawn during the months between April and June. Everyday, on my morning walks with my pet dog, Pixie, I am joined by a group of three mongrels. That day, too, was no different. As Pixie and I came down, the three other dogs accosted us and we began the daily ritual.

We had barely taken a few steps down the fenced promenade of our society when it happened. I had scarcely taken notice of this lean, limping man ahead of me. Suddenly, Pixie and the mongrels ran ahead to the man, surrounded him, nudged him with their noses and welcomed him with a generous wagging of their tails.

Who was this man, I wondered. My curiosity took me closer to the person who, by now, was returning the love showered on him by the dogs, patting them and running his fingers fondly through their wafts of hair. On taking a very close look, I remembered him. He was one of the 16 security guards who used to guard our huge housing society. However, I hadn't seen him for quite a while. On asking him, the man, who was now a pale shadow of his former self, said he had suffered a devastating paralytic attack six months ago and had lost his job. "Life has been very tough, Sir, during the last six months. When in trouble, no one remembers you. No one was willing to help," the man rued. "Sir, no one remembered me in the society. Only the dogs did. They are truly my friends," he said, fondling Pixie. I was speechless, perhaps too abashed at my forgetfulness, an outcome of human insensitivity.

"If you pick up a starving dog and make him prosperous, he will not bite you. It is the principal difference between a dog and a man," said American author, Mark Twain. We have lessons to learn from a dog. Loyalty and gratefulness have long done the disappearing act from the human horizon. We tend to forget people, even those dear to us, so soon. It took me six months to forget the guard I have known for three years, until Pixie reminded me of him. Is this what we have reduced human bondage to?

So, think smart with a heart. Don't forget people. Remember them. You too will then remain in their hearts. ❐

5

Safeguard Self-Esteem, Cut Employee Attrition

"To be yourself in a world that is constantly trying to make you something else is the greatest accomplishment," said American poet, Ralph Waldo Emerson. Few companies seem to have grasped the import of the statement, though. Those that have given due respect to their employees to fan their self-esteem have seen least attrition rates. As in the case of this World Bank-financed project that I saw on a website in 2012.

Four years ago, as part of its corporate social responsibility initiative, Intimate Fashions decided to join the Tamil Nadu Empowerment and Poverty Reduction Project, which was 75 per cent financed by the World Bank with $274 million. The project, called *Pudhu Vaazhvu* ("New Life"), sent 1,800 economically disadvantaged women from 26 districts of Tamil Nadu with only primary school education to work at Intimate Fashions. What I found particularly notable about the project was that it has a clear, hassle-free exit strategy once the current term of operations ends in 2014.

Guduvanchery, 20 kilometers south of Chennai, is home to the Intimate Fashions Factory that makes brassieres.

Intimate Fashions manufactures seven million bras a year, generating a revenue of $40 million. The milieu provided for the workforce at the factory is perfect: Inside the large manufacturing unit in Guduvanchery, peppy Tamil film music plays in the background as women work amid mountains of brightly-coloured bras. The factory now employs 2,500 women over 18 and 92 per cent of them are from families below the poverty line from various districts of Tamil Nadu.

Now, here's the catch: The city of Chennai constantly faces labour shortage as workers keep moving out for just ₹ 100 extra to another company. No less than companies like Nokia and Ford compete for a decent labour force. Amid such stiff competition, Intimate Fashions has managed to retain its employees with minimal attrition rate. The way wasn't hard to traverse. All workers are paid the minimum monthly wage of ₹ 3,500. Post the completion of training which usually exceeds four weeks, they are paid an added incentive of up to ₹ 200 per day. To further pep up enthusiasm, employees get a nutritional hot beverage instead of coffee in the morning since many are anemic.

For a personality makeover, the women are given free training in spoken English and personal grooming. Most women admit that the factory is like a second home (and many hadn't even stepped out of their homes prior to the project).

For the participants, the single most significant benefit of this project is the self-esteem that comes with earning a decent income and independence. As a woman from the factory corroborated in a television interview that after taking up this job, residents from her hometown were showing her more respect. Even her parents now asked for her advice. This all adds up to give her a high that originates from exalted self-esteem.

So, we've got to think smart to appreciate that employees are possessive about their self-esteem. Any attempt to torpedo their dignity and they wouldn't hesitate to move on, even if for a hundred rupees more. Period.

❐

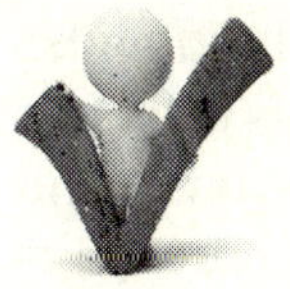

6

Breathe Your Dream to Realise it

The Bharud family was the poorest in Dhule village in Maharashtra. Young Rajendra was told by his mother as a child that his father died just before his birth because the doctors in the village could not save him from malaria. Since childhood, his mother inspired him to become a doctor and save many others from meeting the same fate as his own father.

Wiping off the tears from his mother's eyes, Rajendra knew he had to become a doctor. Somehow…anyhow. Only, he didn't know how. Poverty had subjugated them into near-starvation. Education was like a distant dream.

Time passed by. His mother worked tirelessly to make both the ends meet. Often Rajendra heard his mother and the landlord quarrelling, which eventually his mother almost certainly lost. His mother, Kamal Bharud often grumbled, "I wish I had two children; one, I could have made him a doctor and the other, a police officer to handle these rascals," obviously referring to the oppressive landlord community.

Rajendra was always confused. What should he become—a doctor to save lives or a police officer to handle the "rascals" such as landlords? Some time later, Rajendra's mother got him admitted to a municipal school. Rajendra studied hard, very hard. His guiding force was his teacher's words that he had to score 100 per cent in science and mathematics to become a doctor. His hard work bore fruits and he stood first in the board exams. He then appeared for the medical entrance examinations and scored 194 marks out of 200. This gave him a berth at GS Medical College, KEM Hospital in Mumbai.

On his graduation day, he received the best student award and started serving as a medical intern. He was now Dr. Rajendra Bharud. During his stint, he saw the poor suffer more because of the "uncaring attitude" of the law and order machinery than due to the ailment. He spoke his mind to his dean, Dr. Sanjay Oak, who, in turn, suggested that he take the UPSC exams.

Another battle began, as Dr. Rajendra Bharud borrowed books from other aspirants to prepare for the UPSC. He topped the medical science category, securing an all-India rank of 709. He was selected for the Indian Police Service (IPS).

"The future you see is the future you get," said American author, Robert G. Allen. Dr. Rajendra Bharud is glad to have fulfilled both his mother's wishes, the second more than the first. He is also glad that he often spoke to himself about his plans and got others to give their opinion about how to go about his plans.

So, think smart. To nurture your dream, be a kid. See your future, relish it, talk about it to yourself and your well-wishers. Remind yourself everyday that you need to achieve your goal and all impediments in the way may simply melt away.

❐

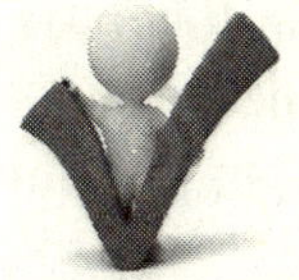

Let the Old Lead the New

I remember the days as a child when my grandmother would recount stories from the Panchatantra, the Ramayana, the Gita or the Mahabharata to put us to sleep every night. The values of life that the stories carried with them touched our hearts and have remained with us to this day.

That, however, is an old story. Grandparents no longer tell such stories to children in which our culture and heritage are pivotal. Youngsters grow up in a materialistic world, efficient in sprouting materialistic ideas, but deficient in values like mutual trust and emotional balance.

This the leading business schools of the country seem to have realised. In order to marry human values to business intelligence, top business schools of the country are including tales from Panchatantra, philosophies of Swami Vivekananda and bits from the Bhagwat Gita, the Mahabharata and the Ramayana and are aiming to dovetail their messages with current business strategies for better, more stable long-lasting results.

Take the instance of the Bharatidasan Institute of Management from Trichy in Tamil Nadu which has tied up with Sri Aurobindo Institute in Puducherry (Pondicherry) to bring the great thinker's teachings within the fold of modern-day management syllabus to endow students with a consciousness that transcends organisational and national barriers. So is the case with IIM, Calcutta, which has launched an executive programme, which includes poetry by Kalidasa and Kautilya Arthashastra. ISB, Hyderabad also conducts leadership transformational programmes, which rely strongly on the wisdom of the Gita.

At the root of all this is the belief that programmes that envelop Indian ethos can enable top managers to handle situations effectively by bringing in a wider perspective. Programmes that draw knowledge from age-old epics have diverse intellectual philosophy, ethics, psychology and culture that help to drive business objectives.

Consider this. Indian culture has it that one can make best use of waste. Interestingly, this has been picked up more by other countries than India itself. Amsterdam has given birth to a new shop idea called "repair café". All household items that are broken or have cracks are fixed free in such cafés. They are then either used by the owners or are given to the needy. To arrest the increasing menace of e-waste, many countries are taking this Indian concept as the guiding principle and are encouraging people to use old electronic items without discarding them. The Dutch Government, with a funding of $ 525,000, is goading people to recycle products and, thus, save the environment. People too have seen reason in this. From retired people to NGOs, all have come together to participate in this extraordinary move and are donating funds to pay for the engineering staff, marketing and running of such 'repair cafés'.

"The old gives way to the new." This is an old saying from the Bible. Old orders will change, new ones will prevail.

But think smart. Remember, the old holds within it the seeds of the new and if the ethos ingrained in the old—like in the case of our epics - is integrated into the new, the new will flourish. Period.

❐

Excellence as a Matter of Habit

A rank of 8,137 in the IIT-JEE examinations is not exactly a great achievement. *Per se.*

Unless you have 12-year-old Satyam Kumar from a farmer's family in Bhojpur district in Bihar notching up the rank in 2012, a precocious child, more important than the rank grabbed by the less-than-a-teenager is the fact that he didn't seem satisfied with his laurels and when interviewed, spoke about studying at a school in Kota, Rajasthan. That, he said, would equip him to take the exams again next year to beat his own score. He said he wished to become the next Mark Zuckerberg and develop a software firm on the lines of Facebook.

Satyam's case takes me back several years, when I met Captain C.P. Krishnan Nair, owner of Leela Hotels, to get a cover story for Indian Express' special magazine called *Express Hotelier and Caterer*. Nair, who built world-class hotels across the length and breadth of the country, retains the same level of enthusiasm today at 90 as he did when he began his enterprise. To this day, he can be seen inspecting the nitty-gritty at, maybe, Udaipur Lake Retreat or Leela Palace in Bangalore, two of the most luxurious hotels in the world.

Nair's career itinerary is quite engrossing. He began his career as an army captain and his first posting was

Abbottabad (where Osama Bin Laden was captured and killed) as a wireless officer and his job was to intercept messages exchanged between two major axis powers, namely Germany and Japan. He took retirement in 1952 and was posted as ADC and principal officer to the Army Commander General, but soon decided to bid goodbye to the army. He then joined his father-in-law's textile industry. His friendship with V.P. Menon, a country cousin and also political advisor to India's last Governor General, Lord Mountbatten, helped him immensely. In 1957, when he was eyeing a bigger opportunity and was in talks with the Scottish firm, Lawrence Mitchell, the latter asked him for a reference from India. So, he called up Menon, but the phone was accidentally picked up by Mountbatten himself. The Governor General was impressed with Nair's enthusiasm and volunteered to speak to Lawrence Mitchell firm himself. The deal was sealed and Leela Scottish Lace Limited went on to become a big name in the field by 1970. Then came the Leela Hotels chain, which redefined hotel luxury on the global map.

"Don't strive to be perfect. Strive for excellence," American actress, Victoria Principal once said. That's because excellence is attainable, unlike perfection. Excellence is not a one-time achievement. It's a constant urge to better oneself without any room yielded to mediocrity.

So, think smart. Once the urge to do better becomes second nature, excellence dons a permanent garb.

❐

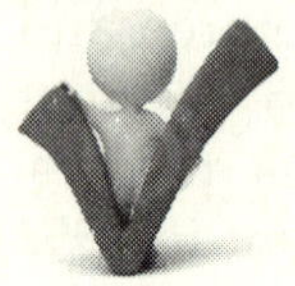

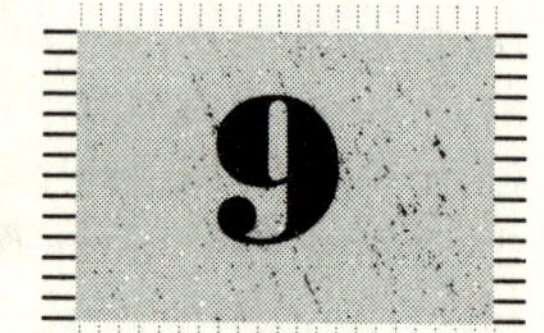

Kids, Trust Your Parents Implicitly

There is one incident I remember with dread and love—in that order - from my college days. It was hot and humid in Mumbai and there was this kid, who had gone for a swim at the lake behind our IIT-B hostel. Ten minutes into a merry swim, the boy failed to see an alligator furtively approaching him.

His father, who worked at the hostel canteen, was passing by when he saw the alligator. Shivering with fright, the man called out to his son and warned him of the predator, who was now a few feet away. The boy swam desperately towards the banks with the alligator in hot pursuit. It was too late, though. Just as the boy reached his father, the alligator also reached him. From the dock, the father grabbed his little boy by the arms just as the alligator dug its teeth into his legs.

Then began, what you may call, an incredible tug-of-war. The alligator was obviously much stronger than the father, but the father was much too passionate to let go. The security personnel, who heard his screams, took aim and shot in the water without hurting the alligator and which made the animal flee. Remarkably, after weeks and weeks at a hospital, the boy survived. His legs bore deep scars left by the vicious attack. And, on his arms were deep scratches where his father's fingernails had dug into his flesh in his effort to hang on to his son in a bid to save his life.

A newspaper reporter, who interviewed the boy after the trauma, asked if he could show him his scars. The boy acquiesced, but was quick to add, "But look at my arms. I have deep scars on my arms too. I have them because my Dad would not let go."

All of us identify with the boy, somehow. There are scars we have—mostly those that leave deep imprints in our memory—that remind us of how our parents, or should I say, the living Gods, have on several occasions brought their being in the firing line in order to save our skin, just as in the case of the boy, who might otherwise have been devoured by the alligator.

A Chinese proverb says, "To understand your parents' love, you must raise children yourself." Kids, please remember, when your parents scar you with their words or actions, they are not doing so for some selfish ends, but because they don't want their dear child's future to wade into unacceptable situations.

So, think smart. Kids, trust your parents implicitly.

❐

10

Be Thankful for Gifts Given

Raj Mehra, a middle-level MNC employee, was on his first trip abroad. He was sent because the company decided to ramp up the thinking process of middle-level employees by exposing them to foreign trips and training. Raj was obviously overwhelmed with joy and gratitude for his boss who had recommended his name for the trip. He thought of buying a gift for him, oblivious though he was of his superior's tastes. He bought a gift, nonetheless, from a store in London, which he thought was decent and upon returning, humbly gave it to his boss. Much to Raj's chagrin, his boss accepted the gift with a phlegmatic smile and tossed it on the sofa beside him with a customary 'Thank you'. Hurt beyond words, Raj never bought a gift for anyone on his subsequent trips abroad. To him, the word 'gift' made no sense anymore.

This reminds me of a story wherein a young man, while roaming in a desert, came across a spring of crystal-clear water. The water was so sweet that he filled some in his leather canteen so that he could bring it back to his tribal elder, who was a teacher. After a four-day journey, he presented the water to the old man who took a deep sip, smiled warmly and thanked his student lavishly for the sweet water. The young man returned to his village happily. Later, the teacher let another student taste the water. He spat it out, saying it was awful. It apparently had become stale because of the old leather container. "Master, the water is foul. Why did you pretend that it was sweet?"

The teacher smiled, "You only tasted the water, my child. I tasted the gift. The water was immaterial. What I found to be really sweet was the feeling of love that accompanied the water, and not the water itself."

This is something of a lesson all of us need to learn. We often fail to see the feelings of a person when he gives us a present. "You give but little when you give of your possessions. It is when you give of yourself that you truly give," said Lebanese-American writer, Kahlil Gibran. It's that bit of intimate *yourself* we must learn to appreciate when we are given a gift. We should remind ourselves and also teach our children about the beauty of gratitude. After all, gifts are an expression of love that emanate from the heart. When we express our gratitude, we must not forget that the highest of appreciation is not to utter a few soft words, but to live by them.

So, think smart. Remember the saying—never look a gift horse in the mouth and say 'thank you' right from the core of your heart.

❒

Acquire New Skills to Excel

The only 'asset' in a manufacturing system whose value can appreciate over time is the human asset. The value of all other assets, including machines, tools and buildings depreciate. That is the reason companies put these items under the depreciation head in their balance sheet, while employee experiences are mapped before the investors.

However, what's integral to making the human asset more valuable is packaging and dusting of the so-called employee. Packaging refers to your outer shell—the way you present yourself. It transcends your appearance. A research by *Harvard Business Review* says that people form snap opinion about you based on your external appearance in the first 15 seconds whether at an interview, a party or a meeting. These impressions are sticky, as it takes eight pieces of positive information to undo an initial negative impression created out of packaging. And that is the filter through which people view you in all your subsequent actions.

There is, therefore, great merit in taking care about the way you present yourself. Good grooming, including accessories like bag, pen, shoes, socks, handkerchief, business card case may not be important individually, but they collectively contribute to the brand called 'you'.

As for dusting, it is nothing but how you communicate at the marketplace. The marketplace starts from your immediate boss to those who matter in identifying you in your hierarchy. Frequent dusting of your knowledge brings greater self-confidence and self-belief. It is about conducting yourself with conviction. If you want people around you to be receptive to the ideas and strategies you bring to the table, then it depends on you how you manage your own brand.

In countries like Japan and Germany, companies have long-term orientation for employee continuity. To them, flexibility in employment means the ability of employees, supported by employers, to learn new capabilities. They seldom dispense with employees who cannot learn new tricks. They identify the core competency in them and put them in different fields.

Employee satisfaction is greater in developed nations compared to an emerging sector like India, where getting a replacement employee is considered to be good for profitability. *Harvard Business Review*, however, says that this attitude generally brings down profitability and productivity over a period of time. Various surveys and studies posit that an employee needs a well-groomed persona, knowledge, packaging and communication skills to be successful. "In order to succeed in life, you need creative skills because look at how fast the world is changing," said American psychologist, Robert Sternberg. To compete with other countries and people, one needs to have a faster learning environment in which both employer and employee must work in concert.

So, employees and employers think smart. As an employee, you must have multiple recipes for being successful in your sphere of work. As for employers, keep chipping off the rough edges of the employees so that they remain useful to you.

❐

There is Life Beyond Divorce

Gone are the days when failure in a relationship meant slipping into a cocoon of self-pity. Now, making a show of a loss is in vogue, where with a bit of innovation and courage, one can help reinvent life after a mishap.

It's happening in the US and elsewhere. A mother and daughter duo, who went through a very bad divorce patch in their life, started an exhibition called "Start over Smart". This means that divorce is not the end of life. Usually, divorce is a tedious process, which leads to enormous emotional and financial drain, not to speak of the stigma it carries in the society. But all that is set to change. You can start life afresh. There are people out there, who will tell you how.

In fact, the first exhibition of this kind was held in Paris in 2010. Here, the daughter-mother pair of Nicole Baras Feuer and Francine Baras started to spread the idea of "Start over Smart". So what's there at the exhibition? The first thing that the mother-daughter duo did was to position the word divorce as a "positive experience". They called it a "new beginning". Apart from stalls selling divorce cakes and divorce rings, there are separate stalls for men and women. The walk-in agencies, that have stalls, help you get speed dating, so that you can forget the bitterness of the past faster. They help you to get online dating too. There are seminars on subjects like "sensuality secrets" and "how to deal with your ex-husband when he calls you", among various other subjects, which might rankle your mind in a state of desperation. You might even have a seminar on "plastic surgery to re-conquer your image".

"Some of us think holding on makes us strong, but sometimes it is letting go," said German-Swiss Novelist, Herman Hesse. The idea of the exhibition is not to make you feel bogged down by an unsavoury event, but to give you hope that it's never too late to bounce back. So, you have "divorce parties" or, maybe, "freedom bash". You have spas, manicurists, nail specialists, acupuncturists, anti-aging treatments, yogis and trips to exotic locations and beaches—all there to make you feel young as if you were a first-timer in marriage.

What comes across is that even a word like 'divorce' can be converted into an industry in which vacation industry, beauty products industry and party industry can all be incorporated to enable and encourage people to reconstruct their life once again.

So, think smart. Life is the greatest of all gifts of nature and far surpasses one unpalatable experience. So, give it a fresh lease with another try.

❐

Go Beyond Call of Duty to Save Lives

One fine day in 1976, Rajkumar Trikannad was piloting the craft TS Cauvery outside Madras Port breakwaters. Some time when the sun was about to set, a squall suddenly broke out. In a few minutes, the sea turned hostile. Rajkumar turned the craft and was returning to the base, when his senior boatswain (Quartermaster), Munnuswamy sighted a fishing craft with three men struggling to stay afloat.

In port management, which is a highly bureaucratic set-up, any action to save civilian life is not attempted, or if done, is a long-drawn procedure and is never reported as it can be seen as jeopardising a government craft.

Anyone else wouldn't have cared, but not Rajkumar and his team of four. The team did not think even for a minute. They reduced the speed, circled around, went back and rescued the three people stuck in the boat. When thanked, Rajkumar felt a bit embarrassed as safety was a priority and a sacred duty ingrained as part of their training. The following year, when Rajkumar met the people he had rescued, one of them said, "Sir, not all captains would have done what you did on that day. Our death was certain. In fact, we dedicate our lives to you."

Another instance comes to my mind. Vanita Kumta, who ran a pathological laboratory in Bangalore, once had a patient who had come in for a blood sugar check-up. The patient's family physician lived just opposite to Vanita's laboratory. The patient never reported that she was a diabetic who had stopped taking her regular medication. However, she had come well armed with an infusion of glucose saying that she was feeling giddy and needed to take it. The doctor sent her to Vanita to check her blood glucose level.

Within 10 minutes, when Vanita saw the readings were well past 250 mgs%, she rushed across the road to tell the doctor about the person's precarious state. Having administered the infusion immediately, the doctor came to the laboratory and thanked Vanita for bringing the report to his clinic and, thus, avoiding a tragic error that could have occurred with the patient having refused to divulge her earlier medical history. Vanita's job, as in the case of any other pathologists, is to keep the report ready and wait for the patient to come and collect it. She, however, exceeded her usual duty and took a call, which, in turn, saved a life.

"Humanity is the greatest of all duties," said Mother Teresa. Be it due to bureaucratic hassles or plain indifference to woes of fellow people, saving lives as a professional code of honourable conduct has lost its identity in the labyrinth of modern-day consumerist priorities.

So, think smart. When executing your professional responsibility, one needs to sometimes stretch and go beyond the call of duty. Your smallest gesture could save a life.

❒

14

Nature Helps Those with a Nice Heart

On one of my trips to Kerala to set-up a news bureau for the Indian Express in the 1990s, I saw a serpentine queue in front of what seemed to be a hardware shop in Ponnani. It did not have a signboard, so I can't tell you the name of the shop. On asking, I was told that it was a hardware-cum-medicine store run by one K.V. Aboobacker, 64.

K.V. distributes medicines free of cost to people who come with prescriptions. This one-man show, known as Aboobacker Self-Service (ABSS), is a boon for many poor patients in Malappuram, Palakkad, Thrissur and Kozhikode districts in Kerala.

K.V. started the service under the aegis of an NGO. Even as he opened a hardware shop in 1971, he began distributing free medicines from the same outlet. He has a wide network of contacts with doctors in five districts. Every week, he goes to hospitals to collect free medicine samples and excess medicines. He stores the medicines in his shop. Medicines that need to be stored at cold temperature are refrigerated at his house.

An unassuming man, who has studied only up to class X, K.V. is immensely knowledgeable about medicines.

Through frequent interaction with doctors and also by reading pharmacology journals, he keeps himself informed about the particulars of medicines, including their dosage, side-effects and expiry dates. In fact, doctors vouch for his reliability.

Patients from distant places are served first, but emergency cases are attended to immediately, even at midnight. K.V. distributes even expensive medicines for heart disease, diabetes and blood pressure. He says the smiles on the faces of the hapless patients are adequate to recompense him for his efforts. Sometimes, when the medicines prescribed are not in stock, he buys them. Each year he spends at least ₹ 50,000 or more on buying medicines. Of course, some donations come his way by way of money contributed by philanthropists. What K.V. says gives him the peg is that his family—wife and three well-settled children—bear no grudge about his spending for ABSS.

K.V. gives away the excess stock to government hospitals and has sent medicines to disaster zones after floods and earthquakes. Doctors respect him and the Indian Medical Association (IMA) has given him a certificate of recognition and requested its members to provide him all possible assistance in his venture.

"Be kind, for everyone you meet is fighting a harder battle," said Greek philosopher, Plato. If you have a compassionate heart and the will to help others in need, resources will come pouring in from various sources. And as the resources come in, your heart will grow softer.

So, think smart. Nature has its way of supporting men on selfless humanitarian missions.

❐

15

Happiness Lies Where the Road to Expectations Ends

Prerna's mother works with one of my relatives in Karnataka as a domestic help. Sometime in 2012, I got a call from my relative asking me to watch a Kannada channel that evening without fail. He explained that Prerna was to be featured on a Kannada version of *Kaun Banega Crorepati* (KBC) on TV that is hosted by cine megastar Puneet Rajkumar.

The entire episode was an eye-opener. Prerna, 24, got selected for the hot seat and, as is the practice, the story of her family was shown in the beginning. She is the second among three daughters and a brother. Born to impoverished parents, the father wanted a son from the beginning. When daughters were born, he started taking it out on the family. So much so that after the third daughter was born, he smashed the infant's head on the wall, maiming her for life. The girl never quite recovered and is still retarded at 20. Ironically, after a son was born, the father abandoned the family, leaving the mother to fend for the kids.

Prerna knew she had to alleviate the woes of her dear ones. Amid teething difficulties, she finished her graduation, but couldn't get her degree certificate from the college due to dearth of money. So, when the channel obtained the certificate from the university and presented it to her as a surprise, she was overwhelmed with emotion.

Prerna went on to win ₹ 3.20 lakhs on the show. The mother and her mentally-challenged daughter appeared on the show as part of the audience. After all the applause, when Puneet asked the younger sister in the audience what she wanted from her sister, Prerna, she said with child-like innocence, "Nothing, but a chocolate." Believe me, I have not seen more moist eyes on a single screen in my life so far.

This set me thinking. If I were in her position, what would I have possibly wanted—maybe my iPhone to be converted to iPhone 4S or a hybrid bicycle—it could be anything fanciful, but a chocolate. The episode was a humbling experience, one that redefined satisfaction for me.

A recent Gallup survey on "satisfaction" has put India in a bad shape. It said the level of satisfaction in India is dipping for various reasons. Employees are generally unhappy during the month when increments are done. Most employees expect the moon and end up disappointed when desires crashland on earth. The truth is, high expectation comes with a package called unhappiness. Author Marty Rubin rightly said, "What is, is plenty, but more is never enough."

So, think smart about a spiritual truth: The pursuit of happiness ends where there is absence of exalted expectations. Period.

❐

16

Being a Mother is a Full-Time, Fully Satisfying Job

A woman wanted to renew her driver's licence at the localtransport office and was asked by the clerk to state her occupation. She hesitated, uncertain of how to classify herself. "What I mean is," explained the clerk, "do you have a job, or are you just a...?" "Of course, I have a job," snapped the young woman. "I'm a mom, I mean a mother."

"We don't list mom as an occupation...housewife covers it," said the clerk emphatically, signed the form and sent her to stand in a long queue. She stood there for three hours, all the while thinking about her second kid, who would remain hungry all this time.

Four years down the line, the same woman, now a mother of three, had a similar opportunity before a clerk at a police station, where she went to get a character certification. The clerk asked in a gruff voice, "What is your occupation?" The young mother hesitated for a while and then said, "I'm a Research Associate in the field of Child Development and Human Relations."

The clerk paused, puzzled and looked up as though she had not heard it right. The mother repeated the title slowly, emphasizing the most significant words. Then she stared with wonder as her pronouncement was written in bold, black ink on the official questionnaire. "Might I ask," said the clerk, "just what you do in your field?" Coolly, with no fluster in her voice, the young mother said, "I have a continuing programme of research (which mother doesn't?), in the laboratory and in the field. (Normally, you and I would have said indoor and outdoor.) I'm working for my Masters, and already have three credits (her three daughters). Of course, the job is one of the most demanding in humanities (no mother will disagree) and I often work 14 hours a day (24 is more like it)."

"But the job is more challenging than most run-of-the-mill careers and the reward is more in terms of satisfaction rather than money," she concluded. Impressed beyond words, the clerk completed the form, stood up and personally ushered the young mother to the door. When she got home, buoyed by her glamorous and newly-described career, the young mother was greeted by her lab assistants, aged 10, 7 and 3. The young mother felt she had triumphed over bureaucracy. She had gone on official records as someone more distinguished and indispensable to mankind than "just another mom or mother".

Novelist Nancy E. Turner had once said, "Motherhood is a girl's highest calling." So, mothers, think smart. Yours is a career where satisfaction is the biggest reward. The world might or might not appreciate it, but the returns are greater than any other profession in terms of satisfaction. ❐

17

Steal Those Little Moments of Happiness

When I was down with severe food poisoning for almost a month and lying in bed some time in 2012, I found pigeons trying to make a nest in my bedroom balcony. As I had nothing to do other than reading books and watching television, I observed something many of us wilfully ignore in the midst of our busy life.

The pigeons collected twigs that were placed in a circular fashion and evidently there was an architectural beauty in it. I chose not to disturb.

Four days later, I found two freshly laid eggs in the nest. Feeling rather tender towards the birds, I brought my glucose drip carton, placed a soft cloth on it and carefully transferred the nest into it when the mother and father were away hunting for food. I was warned that due to this intrusion on my part, the birds might be shocked and may not turn up.

Maybe because they were birds residing in Mumbai, my unsolicited interest did not bother them. Mamma bird would come every hour daily, sit on her eggs to warm them, and who I assumed was papa bird, would stand by and watch. Everyone warned me that pigeons can be a real nuisance. But I could not bring myself to chuck the eggs away, maybe because I was also sick, I was looking for sympathy. Soon the eggs hatched and out came two teenie-weenie baby pigeons, which looked as though someone had combed their feathers backwards. They looked very cute. The mamma and papa bird would come regularly and I would peep and see them actually dropping food into the open beaks of the baby birdies. It was a very cute and touching sight.

Gradually, the baby pigeons grew stronger looked prettier and ventured out by toppling the carton on the side. They shook themselves, looked around grandly, taking in the world as it looked from 10th floor. It had become a lovely pastime of mine, to tiptoe to the French windows and peep out through the glass. I would often find the baby birds dancing or hopping on their tiny feet. When they would hear me opening the door, they would freeze. I could have chucked them away, but I could not because they were still so helplessly small and vulnerable.

Soon they hopped up to near the balcony base skirting, then hopped onto it. Meanwhile, the parent pigeons were regular with their feeding. And then one day, off the birdies flew. I never saw them again, but knew that I had trapped a joyful memory that would remain with me forever.

Life in metros has robbed us of little bits of happiness that were integral to us not so long ago. Caught in the quagmire of a hectic life, we forgo such opportunities to live these moments. I recall what actress Audrey Hepburn once said, "Happiness is health and a priceless memory."

So, think smart and steal those priceless little moments of happiness.

❐

Friends, Enemies of the Unexpected Kind

Enemies, they say, creep up from the unlikeliest of corners. It is an old story that Kodak, the leading camera manufacturing company, never anticipated that its enemy will be a mobile manufacturing company, which will build a camera on the mobile phone.

Who would have thought that Internet would beat television hollow? Imagine, the biggest website boasts of over 60 hours of video being uploaded every minute, over four billion videos being viewed daily, over three billion hours of videos being watched every month, hundreds of millions of new people visiting video sites every month and more videos being uploaded every month than what the three major TV networks in the United States have produced in more than 60 years.

Similarly, when the wine manufacturers complained recently that their business is dwindling and they are going through the worst period in the last ten years, what would be the general perception? Obviously, excess taxation. But that's not the case. All India Wine Producers' Association Head, Jagdish Holkar has gone on record to say that the business is dwindling because the restaurants have less security. Customers have reduced considerably after

26/11 shootout at the Taj Hotel in Mumbai due to fear. The association wants hotels to be treated as a public place and adequate security be provided by the State Governments to increase the confidence in customers.

So much for your unseen enemies. Now, where can your friends be? Companies like Accenture are allowing its employees to share their excess leave with those employees with some untoward emergency. A sudden death, an ailing parent, an accident—these are situations where an employee without any leave may be forced to go on leave without pay. At this time, someone in the company with excess amount of leave can donate his leave to you. This not only creates bonding among employees, but also makes the organisation the best HR practising company.

The point here is that a friend or an enemy in business or at the workplace emerges from unexpected quarters. I quote here what Charles Baudelaire said, "The devil's best trick is to persuade you that he doesn't exist." To catch you unawares is what constitutes the scoring point for a faceless enemy, perhaps the most devious.

So, think and be smart. Friends are fine, but to meet challenges from your enemies, that too, the hidden ones head-on, you need to be on vigil at all times.

❐

SECTION-II

Dream, But be Determined First

19

Will, not Funds, Rings in Success

Gopala Sundara Raj works as a scientist in Jaipur. R.V. Karnan works as an assistant conservator of forest in Maharashtra. Both are 27 and do not know each other. However, their pictures appeared together in leading dailies in the south for successfully competing in the Civil Services examinations in 2012.

Gopala comes from Mavila Thoppu, a tiny village near Kilakarai in Tamil Nadu, whose population is no more than 175 people. His mother, S. Rajammal and father, S. Shanmugavel could not study beyond standards III and V respectively. Both the parents wanted their son to pursue higher education and go to an English-medium school. Poverty, however, stood in the way and Gopala was sent to a Tamil school where education was free.

But Gopala was resolute. He went from strength to strength by the sweat of his brow. Life was as difficult as it could be. Throughout his life, Gopala stayed in a small portion of his maternal uncle's house and his family neither owns any piece of land, nor has any house to stay. Gopala's moral support and motivation was his sister, Sundara Yoga Laxmi, who works with Infosys. Gopala studied under streetlights and at a neighbour's house, which had the power facility. Hard work, sheer determination and dedication finally made him realise his dream.

Cut to the next person. Karnan, who comes from a modest background, was the all-India topper in the Indian Forest Service examinations in 2007. His father, R. Veeraragavan (56) still works as a librarian at Alagappa Arts College and his mother, V. Vijayalakshmi is a sub-registrar in Karaikudi, a small district, 800 kms from Chennai.

Karnan, who never went to a coaching class, feels that competing in the UPSC examinations is all about clearly understanding the methods and patterns of the examinations.

What stands out here is that a modest or low financial background is no impediment for those who have the will to be successful. You do not need coaching classes to make it to your goal. All coaching classes are there in you.

"The man who goes farthest is generally the one who is willing to do and dare. The sure-thing boat never gets far from the shore," said American writer, Dale Carnegie. It's your will and dedication, along with the support of your parents and well-wishers, which propel you to reach your desired destination.

❒

20

Draw Strength from Your Weakness

A 10-year-old boy decided to learn judo despite the fact that he had lost his left arm in a devastating car accident. The boy began his lessons with an old Japanese judo master. The boy was doing well, so he couldn't understand why, after three months of rigorous training, the master had taught him only one move.

"Sensei," the boy finally said, "Shouldn't I be learning more moves?" "This is the only move you know, but this is the only move you'll ever need to know," the sensei replied. "Have faith," the master said.

Not quite satisfied with the answer, the boy continued his training. Several months later, the sensei took the boy to his first tournament and made him clash with normal people who have both arms. Surprising himself, the boy easily won his first two matches. The third match proved to be more difficult, but after some time, his opponent became impatient and charged, but the boy deftly used the one move he had learnt to win the match.

The boy was amazed by his success. He was now in the finals. This time, his opponent was bigger, stronger and more experienced. For a while, the boy appeared to be overpowered. Concerned that the boy might get hurt, the referee called a time-out. He was about to stop the match when the sensei intervened. "No," the sensei insisted, "let him continue."

Soon after the match resumed, his opponent made a cardinal mistake. He dropped his guard. Instantly, the boy used his move to pin him down. The boy had won the match and the tournament.

On the way home, the boy and sensei reviewed every move in every match. Then the boy summoned the courage to ask what was really on his master's mind. "Sensei, how did I win the tournament with only one move?" "You won for two reasons," the sensei answered. "First, you've almost mastered one of the most difficult throws in judo. And second, the only known defence for that move is for your opponent to grab your left arm." The boy's biggest weakness of not having the left arm had eventually become his biggest strength to pin down his opponents.

German statesman, Otto von Bismarck once said, "It is the destiny of the weak to be devoured by the strong. Whether we are weak or strong depends on us." Weaknesses exist in each one of us. It's up to us whether we keep crying over it or whether we turn it into an advantage to beat those much stronger than us.

The message that is driven home here is that each of us is special and important in some way. Only the weak at heart think that they possess some weakness. So, look life in the eye and extract the best out of it.

❐

21

Think a While: How Human are You?

 # Recollection 1: This happened many years ago. In a class test conducted by Dr. S.S. Bhargava of IIT-B as part of our final year of management programme, the last question caught me unawares. "What is the first name of the woman who cleans your building on this campus?"

Surely, this was a joke. I had seen the cleaning woman several times, but how would I know her name? Because it was a class test, I did not care. As I handed over my answer paper, leaving the last question blank, I overheard a student asking the professor if the last question would count in contributing to our total marks. "Absolutely," the professor said. "In your career, you will meet many people. All are significant. They deserve your attention and care, even if what you do is just smile and say hello."

For the next one month, everyone preparing for the final examination ensured that he knew the librarian's name, every peon's name and their responsibility, even the *chaiwala*'s name. We had to prepare ourselves well, should such a "stupid" question be asked again.

In the final examinations, no such question appeared. But today, when we meet up at alumni meets after so many years, we remember all employees by their names. And the same Professor Bhargava stands in a corner, smiling that he had made us that much more human. I've never forgotten that lesson. I also learnt the name of the woman who cleaned our building: Saraswati.

 # Recollection 2: This is an eyewitness account from the New York City. On a cold day in December, a 10-year-old boy was standing before a shoe store on the roadway, bare-footed, peering through the window and shivering.

A lady waiting for a bus approached the young boy and said, "Hey, what are you looking at?" The boy said: "I was asking God to give me a pair of shoes." The lady took him by the hand, went into the store and asked the clerk to get half a dozen pairs of socks for the boy. She then asked the boy to wear a pair and purchased him a pair of shoes. She tied up the remaining pairs of socks and gave them to him. She patted him on the head and said, "Well, you will be more comfortable now." As she turned to go, the astonished kid caught her by the hand and, with tears in his eyes, asked, "Are you God's wife?" The lady said, "No, I am trying to be human after losing my son's leg in a road accident yesterday."

"As human beings, our greatness lies not so much in being able to remake the world—that is the myth of the atomic age—as in being able to remake ourselves," said Mahatma Gandhi. We know we can never become God, nor can we afford to play one. But, at least, we can make ourselves a good human being.

❐

22

Be Instant in Kindness to a Lonely Soul

Sanni was sinking. The pain was unbearable and doctors had given up hope. Conversing was proving to be increasingly difficult. It was the night before August 6. Sanni opened her mouth to speak, but all that came out was a groan. "You want to talk to someone?" asked the doctor-in-attendance. "Yash...in the US," Sanni said, the words made her breathless. Yash...it all seemed like yesterday—August 6—her birthday....

Summer of 2002. Sanjoti Keni Hegde, along with her 7-year-old son, Yash were visiting India for the first time after Yash's birth in the US. It was then that Yash saw her for the first time—Sanni, the servant in his grandparent's house in Bangalore. She hailed from a tiny village in Karnataka and had worked as household help ever since she could remember. Her husband had abandoned her, days after being married, saying she was too ugly. She had no family to speak of and no place to call her own.

One morning, over breakfast and a cup of tea, Yash whispered to his mother, "Mom, when is Sanni's birthday?" She was taken aback for a minute. Although she had known Sanni for so many years, she had never even thought about asking her that. "Why don't you ask her yourself?" she said.

So he did, and, of course, Sanni did not know the date and year she came into this world. In fact, she was amused that someone had asked her this question.

The mother saw Yash became a little quiet after that and later in the evening, he came up to her again and said, "Mom, I believe everybody has to have a birthday and since Sanni does not remember hers, I am going to declare August 6 as her birthday from now on and I am going to hold a little birthday party for her." "Sure," his mother said, thinking that soon Yash would forget about it.

But, no, that little boy went about organising a little birthday party. He got her a cake, her favourite flavour of ice-cream—which happened to be strawberry and which none of the family members knew or had ever thought of asking her. Yash invited a few people and I was part of the party. I even dropped a few hints about what Sanni would like as gifts.

The big day arrived. Yash was so excited. He forced Sanni to sit on the sofa (which she had never done before), made her blow the candles and cut the cake and wonder of wonders, made her eat the first slice herself—again something she had never done before. She unpacked all the gifts, *saris* and trinkets and a huge smile spread across her wrinkled face. Yash then walked up to her, gave her a huge hug and kiss, his big, brown eyes looking into her tired old ones, and said, "I love you, Sanni." That was when the tears fell from her eyes and she quickly wiped them with her edge of her *sari*. "You are supposed to say 'I love you too'," he piped in and she looked at him with a smile and said, "I love you too."

Every night after that, it became a ritual with Yash—he always hugged and kissed her before bedtime and exchanged "I love you." When the time came for Yash to leave India, he made his grandpa promise that he would celebrate Sanni's birthday every year.

Two years following that, however, Sanni developed uterine cancer and was admitted to a hospital. "Her days are numbered," the doctor told Yash's grandpa.

Sanjoti had got the call from the doctor. Sanni wanted to speak to Yash. It was 11 am in the US. Sanjoti didn't think twice. She pulled Yash out of school and put him on the phone. "Hi Sanni, how are you?" Tears rolled down Sanni's cheeks. She wanted to speak, speak and speak a lot. But all she could mumble was, "I love you, Yash." "Love you too, Sanni. Get well soon," Sanni said enthusiastically.

Sanni died the same night....

"If you haven't any charity in your heart, you have the worst kind of heart trouble," said English-born American Comedian, Bob Hope. The small kindness that a little boy showed to a lonely, old woman had made her so happy.... It had lingered on in her heart till her last breath. It is nice to see parents like Sanjoti, who allowed Yash to give those little moments of happiness to Sanni. Most parents wouldn't care. Sanjoti did.

So, if you feel like being kind to someone, be so now.

❐

23

Nothing's More Satisfying than Sharing

Mining workers and their families are possibly the most exploited people in India. Sometime in the 1980s, I happened to accompany one of my friends to his company's inspection laboratory for testing of ores and minerals for exports at a remote mining site in Barytes field at Koduru, a small town in Kadappa district in Andhra Pradesh.

There watching the mining workers and their families was a sad sight. They were somehow clinging on to life. Summer temperatures scorch the arid land and abject poverty is rampant. The limit of acceptance and patience in the struggle for survival is amply seen in the young mothers, rocking their infant children in makeshift cradles tied under a railway wagon in the torrid heat of 40-45 degrees Celsius as they break the ore into smaller lumps with one hand to eke out a living.

At night, after ordering *puri-bhaji* for dinner at a small *dhaba,* I suddenly noticed three waifs who seemed starved. I ordered one more serving for them. I would have expected them to pounce upon the food and devour it. I was surprised, however, that they took the food and left. I was curious. I followed them to a certain distance and saw them join some of their friends, all of them possibly starving. The few *puris* were shared amongst all of them. The most one would have got were a few morsels, but the joy was unbound. They were actually eating a delicacy and more importantly, sharing it among themselves.

Where does such grace in behaviour come from? I wonder. You never see this in metros. The experience left me greatly humbled. Abysmal poverty notwithstanding, the spirit of sharing remained in those kids. I am reminded of what French playwright, Jean-Nicolas Bouilly said, "Whatever we possess becomes of double value when we have the opportunity of sharing it with others."

Life is a gift, the joys of which need to be shared in order to live it to the hilt. Share and see, it not only touches our heart, it also takes away the pressure from the hustle and bustle of the city life.

❐

24

Trust People First, not Technology

It was the first month for an international airline company to introduce swiping system for attendance. The enthusiasm to be 100% perfect for the management ensured that everyone swipes when he or she gets in and exit.

For the first month, the first three days were trial-and-error method, where both swiping and musters were kept, while for the rest of the 27 days, it was made compulsory for all cadres of employees to swipe the card.

At least 45 days into the new system, news about the death of a lowest cadre worker due to heart attack created turbulence in the whole management. The death was not as significant as was the way of dying. He attended to his duties all 31 days in March 2012. When he got his salary, he was shocked to know that the attendance muster showed that he was absent for 28 days, while the three days of salary had been adjusted against other compulsory deductions. So, the employee got no salary that month.

First, he consoled himself that there must be an error and approached the management armed with necessary letters. The management flatly refused to entertain anything saying that swiping the card was a must to prove the presence of the employee in the premises. The only contention of the management was that when each of the 1,387 employees could swipe and get their salary, how come this employee alone managed to dodge the system?

Although his immediate supervisor told him to have patience and was ready to directly take the issue with the right authority and get him the interim benefit, the employee suffered a heart attack and died the same day.

When his swiping card was presented to the management for claiming his final settlement, they found out that the card given to him was a dummy card and not the coded card that would store all information about the employee. Since the dead employee kept swiping the card in the system, the system did not record anything because there was no information in the card itself, thus making no attendance mark for the said employee.

There is a book called *Isaac's Storm*, written by Erik Larson, who is known for his best-selling book *The Devil in the White City*. *Isaac's Storm* is the true story of Isaac Cline, a dedicated employee of the US Weather Bureau and his experience of the hurricane that struck Galveston, Texas in 1900. It was one of the deadliest natural disasters of all times in the United States and the complete city was wiped off the maps and more than 5,000 people were killed. The author explains in that book that despite having a primitive technology, the employees did a pretty good job of tracking the storm. But it failed because the bosses believed in technology and not the employees. Such is the false sense of security generated by our advanced technologies, the book concludes.

"The best way to find out if you can trust somebody is to trust them," said American author, Ernest Hemingway. So, make use of technology, for sure, but trust employees first.

❐

25

Change Yourself to Tame Adversity

A young woman went to her mother and told her how the goings-on were so hard for her. She did not know how she was going to make it and wanted to give up. She was tired of fighting and struggling. It seemed as if when one problem was solved, a new one arose.

Her mother took her to the kitchen. She filled three pots with water and placed each on high fire. Soon the pots came to a boil. In the first, she placed carrots, in the second she placed eggs, and in the last, she placed ground coffee beans. She let them sit and boil, without saying a word.

In about 20 minutes, she turned off the burners. She fished out the carrots and placed them into a bowl. Next, she took out the eggs and placed them into the bowl. Lastly, she put the coffee into the bowl.

Then, turning to her daughter, she asked, "Tell me what you see." "Carrots, eggs and coffee," she replied. Her mother brought her closer and asked her to feel the carrots. She did and noted that they were soft. The mother then asked the daughter to take an egg and break it. After pulling off the shell, she observed the hard-boiled egg. Finally, the mother asked the daughter to sip the coffee.

The daughter tasted its rich aroma. The daughter then asked, "What does all this mean, mother?"

Her mother explained that each of these objects had faced the same adversity: boiling water. Each reacted differently. The carrot, after being subjected to the boiling water, softened and became weak. The egg had been fragile. Its thin outer shell had protected its liquid interior, but after sitting through the boiling water, its inside hardened. However, the ground coffee beans were unique. After they were left in the boiling water, they had changed the water. "Which are you?" she asked her daughter.

When adversity arrives, how do you respond? "Are you a carrot, an egg or a coffee bean?" Think: Which am I? Am I the carrot that seems strong, but with pain and adversity, wilts and becomes soft? Am I the egg that starts with a malleable heart, but changes with the heat? Or am I like the coffee bean? The bean actually changes the hot water, the very circumstance that brings the pain. When the water gets hot, it releases fragrance and flavour.

"Adversity causes some men to break, others to break records," said American writer, William Arthur Ward. Think: When things are at their worst, can you change the situation around you? How do you handle adversity? Are you a carrot, an egg or a coffee bean? That's food for thought.

❐

Education, the Cornerstone of Good Life

Most of us wouldn't like to be sandwiched between unknown people onboard a flight. Would the people on both sides be irritating, you would think. On one of my flights in 2012, I got to sit between a senior woman aged 72 and a sad-looking middle-aged man aged about 50.

Much to by delight, however, the experience I shared with them was exhilarating.

One of the ladies introduced herself as Madhuri Thathachari, a retired research data manager from the University of California, who runs a trust called Bhramara Trust of YT in Mysore, Karnataka. Apart from helping people who lose their family members during natural disasters every year, she helps various institutions across the nation to identify the good work of scientists in their respective streams and felicitates them by presenting an award in the memory of her husband, Professor Y.T. Thathachari, who was a renowned scientist and scholar.

Madhuri gives a cash prize of ₹ 1 lakh to deserving scientists to promote and create interest among the youth in the field of research and development. She also organises Carnatic music competitions (with free entry) to provide a platform to youngsters. She has also instituted an award in the name of legendary Carnatic vocalist, M.S. Subbulakshmi. She is also planning a veterinary hospital in Mysore so as to provide treatment to stray dogs and cattle.

The best thing is Madhuri does not raise funds to help the needy, but uses her own resources for the purpose. She helps underprivileged students by paying fees for courses like engineering and nursing, besides helping patients suffering from cancer and heart diseases. She told me she could do all this because her children who are well-settled abroad have told her not to leave any money for them and spend her savings for good causes.

On the other seat next to me was Asutosh, director, primary education, Bihar, who said he had signed over 150 sacking letters some days ago. He lamented the fact that there weren't adequate quality people in the field of education. He apparently sacked over 150 teachers because when they were tested for their knowledge of English, Mathematics, Hindi and General Knowledge for up to Class 5, they failed miserably. He told me he had asked his junior officials in various districts to comply with the order which allows all teachers to be tested in certain parameters during the next fortnight. He said that many more may lose their jobs, but he was committed to giving the next generation the best of teachers possible.

I kept thinking about my two co-passengers – one wants good teachers, while the other wants good education to be encouraged. I connected the dots. Yes, ultimately, the foundation for the next generation is education.

"Education is the most powerful weapon which you can use to change the world," said former South African President, Nelson Mandela. Look around. There are examples galore which corroborate that if one has a good foundation in education, his life would never be on an unstable ground.

❐

27

Perceptions can Ruin. Be Objective

Ganesh (name changed), while leaving for New Delhi where he was transferred from his hometown in Gujarat, never imagined his life was destined to turn topsy-turvy. A thoroughly organised person by nature, Ganesh was a bit too meticulous about managing his finances. His credit card had his wife, Laxmi (name changed), as the second card-holder.

It so happened that whenever Laxmi went out to shop with the credit card, Ganesh, who would be tipped off on his mobile by the bank about the expenditure, would call his wife to enquire what she had bought and whether the amount mentioned on his mobile was correct. He did not mean any harm, but his persistent nature in enquiring about the slightest expense began to rub on Laxmi irritatingly.

With time, the perception grew on Laxmi that Ganesh was acting cheap. At one of the kitty parties, she remarked, "Ganesh nowadays has become a miser like his father," a statement that was overheard by Ganesh's father.

When Ganesh came to know this, he chided Laxmi for behaving in a childish manner. Laxmi was livid. The rift kept widening. Eventually, things came to a pass when the two decided to separate and go their own ways.

Some time later, Ganesh's father died in Ahmedabad. Ganesh flew down to do the last rites. The COO of the local branch attended the funeral which was at 12 noon. There was no other person from the company who came for the funeral as they were not aware of the death. After attending the funeral, the COO went home, had a shower, changed and came back to office after lunch and started working quietly. He told his secretary that the staff members be informed about Ganesh's father's death after working hours so that they could visit him at his home on their way back to their respective homes.

The COO was of the opinion that if he had broken the news at 12 noon, half the office would have taken a break to either go to meet Ganesh or would have gossiped about his marital dispute, which anyway would have been unproductive.

That was, however, not what the members of the staff thought. They thought the COO was rather inhuman in having kept the news of the death to himself. Else, they could have attended the funeral of a colleague's father.

"Change the way you look at things and the things you look at change," said renowned author, Wayne Dyer. One needs to understand that some decisions have to be taken after considering how it would be perceived by the receiver of the message. If you are a good leader, stand on the other side, receive the message and then analyse what the receiver might think. Then, take an appropriate decision. ❐

28

Inclusive Growth must for a Stable Society

There is a story of an anthropologist who was studying the habits and customs of an African tribe. Most of the time, he found himself surrounded by children. So, he decided to play a little game with them. He got some candy and put them all in a decorated basket at the foot of a tree.

Then he called the children gathered there and said, "Let's play a game. When I say 'now', you have to run to the tree and the first one to get there can have all the candy." When the anthropologist said "now", all the children took one another by the hand and ran together towards the tree. They all arrived at the same time, divided the candy among themselves and began to happily munch away.

The anthropologist asked them why they ran together when one of them could have all the candy to himself. One of the children said, "But sir, what about Ubuntu? How can one of us be happy when the rest are all feeling sad?"

Ubuntu is a philosophy of the African tribes that can be summed up as "I am what I am because of who we all are." South African activist, Bishop Desmond Tutu gave this explanation in 2008: "One of the sayings in African country is Ubuntu, which is the essence of being human. Ubuntu speaks particularly about the fact that you can't exist as a human being in isolation. It speaks about our interconnectedness. You can't be human all by yourself, and when you have this quality – Ubuntu – you are known for your generosity. We think of ourselves far too frequently as just individuals, separated from one another, whereas you are connected and what you do affects the whole world. When you do well, it spreads out and it is for the whole of humanity."

It is becoming difficult for the fenced society like ours to consider the commonality of life themes in every human group, religion and philosophy. Whatever may be the apparent or hidden or even superficial differences among the people of the world, we have to be truly 'Ubuntu'.

"Sometimes, reaching out and taking someone's hand is the beginning of a journey. At other times, it is allowing another to take yours," opined science-fiction writer, Vera Nazarian. Inclusive growth of all communities is the only survival method for a stable society. Think of others, make them grow and you will see societal ills nose-diving. Inclusive growth will help us bond better, while isolation will only create a mentality to disrupt and destroy.

❐

Hone, Nourish the 'X Factor' in You

One often wonders, "What's this 'X Factor' that people often talk about?" What is it that endows a person with this so-called 'X Factor'? Does it mean one is different from others? Does it make him more special? Is he more endearing and daring than others? Does he stand out in the crowd?

Yes, it's all these factors and more, perhaps, that we collectively call 'X Factor'. There is nothing specific about this 'X factor' — it may be a particular way of talking, a smile, or a caring gesture or just a look in the eyes or even an attitude. Each of us is endowed with that 'something'. Search and you shall find it within you. Thereon, one just develops that quintessential quality to attain greater heights of perfection.

There was a popular talent show on television called "The X Factor". The judges studied different contestants and tried to figure out who had that indefinable 'something' that made him unique. Watching the show, I found one couldn't definitively put his finger on it. It's not just talent, looks or personality. There was something about them that gave them an advantage. I remember the judges say, "I don't know what it is, but you've got it." They called it the "X Factor". And that's what it is—'X', the unknown quality.

In one of my interviews with the Kanchipuram Muthu Swami Chandrashekar, he said, "In the same way, when God breathed His life into you, He put something in you to give you an advantage in this life. There is something about you that makes you stand out, something that draws opportunity, something that causes you to overcome obstacles, to accomplish dreams. You are before me to take an interview because you can write and that is the reason I am spending time with you. That is your quality," he concluded.

British author, George Bernard Shaw, once describing the inner struggles of the human race, said, "Inside of me, there are two dogs. One is mean and evil. The other is sane and good. The mean dog fights with the good one all the time." When asked which dog wins, Shaw reflected for a moment and then replied, "The one I feed the most."

Everyone has this 'X Factor'. All you need to do is to identify it. It's up to you then how you develop it to your advantage to achieve your dreams.

It would be smart to think the way Shaw thought and put it before us. It's up to you how much you feed this good dog called 'X Factor' to reach the zenith.

❐

There is Always Light at the End of the Tunnel

It was an occasion worth remembering. Some years ago, a friend who has a factory that produces the finest Bone China Crockery in north Delhi, held a photo exhibition on how India has been producing such materials for the last three centuries.

At the entrance of the exhibition was placed a huge statue of Lord Buddha. We had several rounds of deliberations, at the end of which we wrote two stories, framed them and displayed them for all to read. The stories went thus:

 # Story 1: This is the story of a beautiful red tea cup made of clay. The creator put a lot of efforts into making it. He rolled it, patted it over and over, spun it around the spinning wheel and then put it in the oven and caused it to burn. Then the creator brushed and painted it all over causing the tea cup to suffocate in the fumes and then kept it in an oven twice as hot. When he was satisfied, he handed over a mirror to the tea cup and asked it to see if it looked good. The tea cup could hardly believe itself to be so beautiful.

Then the creator said, "I know it hurts to be rolled and patted, but had I left you, then you would have dried up. I know it made you dizzy to spin around on the wheel, but if I had stopped, you would have crumbled. I knew it hurts as it was hot in the oven, but if I hadn't put you there, you would have cracked. I knew the fumes were bad when I brushed and painted you all over, but if I hadn't done that, you would not have hardened and would not have any colour in your life. Now you are a finished product. You are what I had in mind when I first began with you."

 # Story 2: This is from the Gospel of the Buddha. There was once a woman named Kisagotami, who was stricken with grief and wanted the Buddha to relieve her of pain. The Buddha told her, "Fetch me a handful of mustard seeds and your happiness shall be returned to you. Only the seeds must come from a family that has not grieved ever." Kisagotami went from door to door in the whole village asking for the mustard seeds, but everyone said, "Oh, there has been so much grief here." Kisagotami could not find a single household that had not been visited by grief.

Finally, Kisagotami returned to the Buddha and said, "There is grief in every family. Now I understand your teaching." The Buddha said, "No one can escape unhappiness. If people expect only happiness in life, they will be disappointed."

Helen Keller once said, "We could never learn to be brave and patient if there were only joy in the world." Author, Kahlil Gibran put it thus: "Your joy is your sorrow unmasked. The deeper that sorrow carves into your being, the more joy can you contain. Joy and sorrow are inseparable."

Think of it: Joy and sorrow come together. When one sits with you, the other is asleep. That is the reason our ancestors said that there is always light after darkness.

❐

Tap the Non-Expressive Rural Market

What is common between an alphonso mango grower in the Konkan belt, an orange grower in Nagpur, an apple grower in Kashmir and a potato grower in some part of eastern India? If you think that they are all farmers basically growing and selling their products and making money, you are right. But just about partially. You have missed out on an important factor, perhaps given their rural background. And that factor is 'ASPIRATION'.

To come to think about it, rural aspirations are as high and swanky as urban India's. The only difference is in the lack of expression. People in villages aren't articulate about their deep-rooted desires. They want somebody to come to their place and talk about them. After having a house, family and a reasonable amount of money to lead a good life and that too in a clean environment, they too desire to own a car and drive it through the orchids with their wives seated beside them. However, not many understand this.

One company that has taken this buried aspiration seriously is Maruti Suzuki. They converted a Tata truck into a small mobile theatre, took it to villages and made villagers watch a 13-minute capsule film on Maruti Suzuki. The truck had a split AC, push-back chair and Samsung large LCD screen. After the movie, mimicry artistes came before them, cracked jokes on famous Bollywood stars and asked questions from films. People who answered the questions correctly got a cap, pen or small gifts with logos of Maruti.

The film shown to them has a simple storyline: An average villager, who after succumbing to the persuasive skills of his friend who owns a Wagon R, ends up buying one for himself. It's driven by a simple plot and has identifiable characters, all of whom are average farmers and their sons.

Earlier, tapping rural market was not on the radar of many marketers. But the auto industry is now traversing the national highways to get the attention of the bylanes of the hinterland. Today, it has become the main business as 65% of its consumers are from the rural market and they have high aspirations which they are not talking about. What these marketers do is fuel the villagers' aspirations, which eventually gets converted into sales.

The basics here are straight cut: Aspirations are the same for the rural and the urban markets. "You cannot demonstrate an emotion or prove an aspiration," said British statesman, John Morley. One needs to understand the aspirations of the rural folk. While villagers shy away from making their aspirations public, the urban folk flaunt them. It is up to marketers how well they can tap this non-expressive, yet high aspiration rural market.

❐

32 Unconditional Love of the Canine Kind

Death has been close to me. Five deaths every 10 years during the last five decades, where I have seen five of my favourite pet doggies die in my lap, is close enough. While caressing them on their head before they departed for their last journey, I could see their moist eyes just before they closed forever.

Moti, Ceasu, Kunju, Dada and Snowy—all died with their head on my lap. I remember all those five cruel nights. Those nights have taken away the best of my life. The last of the deaths—of Ceasu—was particularly heart-wrenching. He did not shut his eye the whole night and neither did I. Too weak to move, his strength had been drained out due to not eating for a month and rising creatinine count.

It was about two in the morning when Ceasu vomited bile and saliva and looked at me as if he was bidding the last goodbye. I tried feeding him water, but he spilled it out. I knew his last moment had come. The end came about three hours later. My wife poured some *ganga jal* into his mouth and prayed for a while before we took him to the electric crematorium.

As a management *guru*, I always advocate that all things subjective can be measured. I argue and I win. But I have always failed when it comes to measuring the unconditional love that dogs have for their masters. I know not how to measure Ceasu's love showered by the wagging tails. I will always miss the way he wriggled between my feet when I returned from work or from a long tour. I will miss the way he sniffed my suitcase to see if I had got something for him. I will miss the way he glared at me jealously if I ever showed my love for any other dog. They are so possessive about their masters and don't like sharing their masters with anyone, though they wouldn't mind sharing their food with the stray dogs in the colony.

Whenever I see people fighting with that Kolaveri Di rage, ready to go for one another's throat, I get this feeling that some day I should tell them what love is, what it means to love unconditionally. Maybe, they can learn it from the dogs rather than men who seem more blood-thirsty than ever. No wonder, French statesman, Charles De Gaulle opined, "The better I get to know men, the more I find myself loving dogs."

❐

Teach Children to Respect Money

There are two incidents that come to my mind. The first happened years ago. I was standing at an eatery in Mumbai when I happened to hear an affluent woman shrieking at her 11-year-old son for having overspent on his birthday party while treating his classmates. The deal, I eavesdropped, was that the boy would treat 10 of his classmates to pizzas costing ₹ 150 each. The sum was simple. Thus, the mother gave him ₹ 1,500.

Upon reaching the eatery, the children were tempted with the 'combo offer' which apparently comes with an aerated cola and garlic bread. This jacked up the bill to ₹ 2,000. As the boy was running short of money, he had to seek his mother's help to bail him out of the financial imbroglio. When asked why he spent more, the boy said argued that by spending just ₹ 200 instead of ₹ 150, he derived more pleasure and more value for money. The boy was oblivious of the gross profligacy, which the mother was rightly trying to drill in.

Now, the second incident. Some 40 years ago, something similar happened to me. My mother gave me five paise (many of you may not have even seen the coin) because I wanted to have a ride on the merry-go-round which would cost me three paise. The owner of the merry-go-round gave me a tempting offer for a second round for two paise. I accepted the discount with pride, because I thought I had saved one paisa and could enjoy another round. Back home, I was thrashed black and blue for taking a decision of spending two 'extra' paise without prior authorisation.

I might have felt bad on that day, but when I look back today, I realise that the thrashing taught me an important lesson on 'educated buying decision'. Money management is a skill which comes from real experience. It is very important that children learn the value of money and the role it plays in our lives. Never spend your money before you have earned it, said America's founding father, Thomas Jefferson. If children are not taught to respect money, they are bound to repent some day.

So, it's time parents thought smart to tell their children to be penny-wise. There is no harm in a bit of indulgence once in a while, but as they say, money too has its limits and happy are those who have understood this secret.

❒

34

Look Beyond the Obvious

On a visit to Jammu sometime in 2012, the J&K DGP, Ashok Bhan gave me what I thought was an excellent idea on how to combat terrorism. He told me we haven't been able to hurt the terrorists where it hurts the most. "We have done very little in that area," he said, citing funds as the most critical area for counter-terrorism initiatives. He listed Hawala, extortion, counterfeiting currency, voluntary contribution and money from infiltrators as conduits from where the money is transferred for terrorism. "If we take stringent measures to arrest this cash flow, terrorism will not get its oxygen to survive," he opined. He was bang on target, I believe.

Another incident comes to my mind. Two agencies, after making numerous trips to a school principal office for three months to sell psychometric test for 300 students appearing for the 10th standard examinations, came over to me and asked how to get the principal out of the bureaucratic situation. I suggested they approach the tuition teachers or coaching classes. They make a better impact on the children because parents perceive a tutorial class that charges around ₹ 40,000 per annum better than a school that charges ₹ 15,000 for the same period. The agency went to the coaching classes and all school students got themselves enrolled for psychometric test in two weeks.

I was once told by some members of the people of my colony that there was a sudden rise in cat menace and the vicinity was full of rotund, healthy-looking felines. I told them to check the drainage system of the complete colony and to our surprise, we found that the 15-year-old drainage had virtually collapsed due to constant movement of trucks during construction time and this had given space to rats to breed. Thus, cats had a gala time feeding on fresh rat meat and were fast putting on weight.

I mentioned all three incidents because they take us away from the obvious. Most of the time, our mind gets conditioned by circumstances that we cannot see beyond the obvious. We start assuming that things are too complicated and are thus haunted by the ghosts of their thoughts, unnecessarily.

"There is nothing as deceptive as an obvious fact," said novelist, Arthur Conan Doyle. We fail to realise that the solution to many torturous problems lies in what the eyes cannot see at one go. So, train your brain to look beyond facades.

❐

35

People in Need Do Need You

Some years ago, in the midst of a conversation, a friend of mine made a generalisation that put me off. He was pissed off with the medical fraternity after his octogenarian father, a heart patient, was given a raw deal by an eminent cardiologist. With a sardonic tinge in his voice, he quoted American statesman, Benjamin Franklin, who said, "God heals and the doctor takes the fees." It certainly hurts when your near ones are not treated well, particularly by doctors. However, generalisations aren't in good taste all the time. To prove my point, I gave him two examples of doctors who, I believed, would prove him wrong.

In the first case, I quoted a newspaper article I saw some years ago where world-renowned cardio-thoracic surgeon Dr. Taweesak Chotivatanapong from Thailand flew all the way to KEM Hospital in Mumbai to operate upon a 10-year-old girl with a congenital disorder. All free of cost. Dr. Chotivatanapong's altruistic gesture had a rationale: the girl was barely 10 and could perhaps savour another 80 years of natural life if saved.

In the second instance, one Hitkishore Dhengula, 94, went to Dr. C.V. Swami Shreedhar in Indore with a hearing problem. Dr. Shreedhar instructed his assistant that the fees be returned as he never charges patients who are 90 and above. He also gave a heavy discount on the hearing aid he gave Dhengula.

The two examples, I explained to my friend, stand out as stark examples of how some medical practitioners still attach importance to their social responsibility, on how to give back to the society which helped them earn fame and lucre. What's more striking in Dr. Shreedhar's case is that he was extending his munificence to nonagenarians who many dismiss as they have entered the fag-end of life's autumn. To respect audacity as much as the innocence of childhood is a rare observance and the Indore-based doctor did exactly that.

Placing the logic on to a wider canvas, shouldn't we all take a leaf out of the book of the two doctors? Isn't it incumbent on all of us to do whatever we can to help those deprived of basic facilities? Social activist, Elizabeth Cady Stanton said, "The happiest people I have known have been those who gave themselves no concern about their own souls, but did their uttermost to mitigate the miseries of others."

Think of it: We don't need to walk the extra mile. A yard or less travelled by each one of us to help those in need can collectively make life's bumpy ride a lot smoother.

❐

36

Relish Humour in Life

Allow me to recount two incidents during railway travel. Most people would admit that train travel is scary, given the vagaries passengers are often subjected to. So was one year ago, when I travelled from Howrah to Bolpur via Shantiniketan, with more than a hundred sheep as company crowding a local train compartment. Initially, I was stunned. Later, when I perceived that travelling with the four-legged creatures could actually be a pleasure, the nauseating feeling gave way to sheer pleasure. In fact, throughout the journey, I fondled a tiny lamb which cuddled up on my lap.

That brings me to my second experience when, in 1979, I took a trip from Chennai to Mumbai after attending a Sadaabhishekam Ceremony (80 years of togetherness in matrimony) of my octogenarian grandparents. An ingenious idea was thought of where 68-odd members of the family booked the return journey in one bogey so that 36 hours on the tracks could be spent without boredom. As for meals, it was decided that instead of food packets, individual food items would be carried in separate plastic buckets to enable a wedding-style lunch and dinner onboard.

All thoughtful planning was torpedoed at the eleventh hour as the reserved coach was cancelled and the 68-strong battalion was separately accommodated in the rest of the

18 compartments, all next to the toilet-berth numbers 73 to 75. The nauseating stink notwithstanding, what worried us was that the food packed in several buckets, was now spread out over 18 bogies. The trains in those days did not have vestibules. So, members carrying the curd-rice bucket had no access to pickles and those with sambar-rice were left without *papads*. Thus began a kind of steeplechase for youngsters among the lot, who got down at every station and exchanged buckets among the bogies. Meals we did have, but piecemeal, served cold, with *papads* tasting like plastic.

Anybody forced through the grind would shoot off on a journey of excoriation against the vicissitudes of the railway masters. Not that I didn't. Later though, I discovered the funny side to the incidents that will remain with me. Forever.

I remember having read an article by eminent columnist, Khushwant Singh that people today have forgotten to laugh. We live in difficult times. American author, Ernest Hemingway once said, "It is in the oddities, the seemingly prickly issues that life offered its best humour." One who can separate the humour from the chafing rigmarole of the daily grind lives the happiest. Agreed, it is not possible to be optimistic at all times, but an effort to spot the funny amid the grumpy makes life that much less pricklier.

❑

37 Note Down Expenses Save on Pocket Money

This might sound a bit of a tall call, but a yoga teacher in Salem, Tamil Nadu, has managed to bring down pocket money expenses of all his students by 50% in just six months. Now, before you refute the fact, let me elaborate. The teacher, K. Ganapathi first asked all his students to write down the pocket money they get to spend in a month. Later, he asked them to specify every paisa they spend on different items. He never told them on what items they should spend.

Every student followed his instruction ritually. The book-keeping exercise continued for two months and they came back to him with their 60-day accounts. They had all spent their money in something or another. Some spent it on chocolates, biscuits, snacks, cold drinks and films. While some said they spent 80% of their pocket money on films, some said they spent 75% on chocolates. Some said their choice was junk food (without which they could have easily lived).

Ganapathi meticulously calculated and made a PoP and MoM analysis of every expenditure chart. In management, product on product analysis is called PoP analysis and month on month analysis is called MoM analysis. Having done both the analyses, Ganapathi showed his students how much they were spending on each item every month. He also showed them an expected expenditure on that item for 12 months.

This technique of book-keeping surprised students who were hitherto oblivious of how they were actually squandering away their money. They got to know where their money was going. In the next two months, they saved their money by keeping away from unnecessary areas. In fact, they saved to the extent that many could even lend money to their fathers during the month-end. Some could even buy bicycles at the end of four months. "That all because a fiscal discipline had set in," explained a proud Ganapathi.

"Too many people spend money they haven't earned, to buy things they don't want, to impress people they don't like," said actor Will Smith. His words ring true when you think of it. To spend is easy. To save is difficult. This is one caution we would all do well to remember. In fact, inculcate the habit of book-keeping for every activity. Or in management terms, keep doing PoP and MoM analysis for everything. A lot of improvement is possible once you have the statistics before you.

❐

38

Small can be Big

I remember an incident involving the English industrialist and founder of Virgin Group, Richard Branson, who, on one of his visits to South Africa, was approached by a few middle-aged women who asked him to lend them money to buy a sewing machine. Branson was impressed with their upfront request, and thought $300 wasn't much for him, but might help the women.

Three months later, Branson was invited to the same place to inaugurate some community projects supported by Virgin Unite, the charitable wing of the Virgin Group. While there, six women gifted him exquisite cotton pillows and tribal clothes which they had made with the $300 he had lent them. A speechless Branson couldn't have asked for a greater reward in terms of satisfaction.

Speaking of satisfaction, my wife and I have been supporting the education of two girls from Amravati in Maharashtra for about six years, paying only ₹ 6,000 per annum for both. What we get in return every year is their progress report and recent pictures. Watching the girls grow in the pictures we've gotten over the past six years, gives us ineffable contentment. If one were to think about it, what have we really done? Nothing, frankly, but our token gesture may help the forsaken girls stand on their own feet.

They might not remember us tomorrow, but they will stay dented in our memories forever.

We often fob off humanitarian deeds, saying only the affluent can afford to help, which is a misconception. Let's say I'm not rich. Nevertheless, can't I save a little, I repeat, only a little from my daily expenses and contribute? It's not just me, you can too. Many a little put together makes a lot, just as many drops coalesce to make an ocean. Each one of us matters. It is the greatest of all mistakes to do nothing because you can do little. Your little can inspire many, and what inspires can never be small. This reminds me of a line from William Shakespeare's *The Merchant of Venice*: "How far that little candle throws his beams, so shines a good deed in a naughty world."

The act of donating a little to make the lives of many a lot easier is not overwhelming. It is as simple as it can be, provided we want it to be so. I have no intention to rattle you by saying that you must make sacrifices to help others. All I am saying is that a little effort, that hardly amounts to any hardship really, can help alleviate the hardship of many. Mother Teresa once said that we as humans can't do great things, only small things with great love.

❒

SECTION-III

Seek Answers From Deep Within

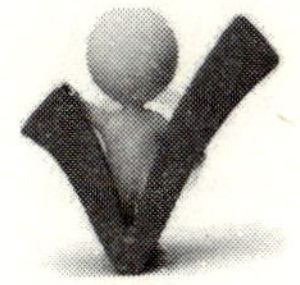

39

Joys of Selfless Service

Let me introduce couple duo, Jugraj Singh Gill and Gurdev Kaur. They belonged to one of the 10 richest landlord families in Moga in the Malwa region of Punjab. Both were MLAs in the early 1970s and held other government positions. They had two sons, one an Indian Air Force pilot and the other a bright college student. Despite being surrounded by pelf and power, both Jugraj and Gurdev were kindness personified. Shorn of even a waft of high-handedness, the caring duo treated acquaintances, including servants, as part of their family. Life, however, was unfair to them. In the early '70s, tragedy drove a wedge into their lives, as both their children perished in grisly tragedies, that too in quick succession. The world came crashing down on them. "We would have fallen irretrievably into an abyss of despair had it not been for Gurdev who suggested we resurrect our love for our sons by reaching out to those left bereft of compassion," I remember Jugraj telling me.

The couple sold off several acres of farmland and buildings to raise money to buy 25 acres of land on the Chandigarh-Ludhiana Road near the township of Kharar. Thus was born a modern old-age home for the elderly, which they named Mata Gurki Sukhnivas. All expenses for this institution are met through a corpus created by the couple, who believe that by sharing the grief with the 200 members at the home, they mitigate their own sorrow. "Sharing the losses of many is better than wallowing in the wilderness of personal loss," said Jugraj. His words still ring in my ears.

I am reminded of what Rocky Balboa said in the cult Hollywood classic 'Rocky', "Real love is when you become selfless... you are now a giver, instead of a taker." Selflessness, if you were to distance yourself from the matrix of platitudinous big talk, is easier said than practised. More so if the acts of selfless service emanate from personal loss, where instead of recoiling into - taking a cue from Shakespeare - "a cocoon of self-deprivation," one makes a tragedy the conduit to spread some moments of joy.

When somebody is in need and we're open, there comes an impulse from inside us. It's at that instant in time when we must choose to act upon it, or the moment tends to go by in a flash. In these turbulent times, we must not let go of that nano-moment urge to do something for others. We must act. Now, more than ever.

❏

40

Observe and Understand

There is an old saying that in the land of the blind, the one-eyed man is king. It's one of those maxims that is universally acknowledged for its truth, and yet, equally ignored. After all, don't most people have two eyes? Well, the saying isn't about whether you have eyes or how good your sight is but it's about how well you use the gift of sight. We all have the tendency to unconsciously ignore information available to our senses.

And we have to do this to continue functioning, otherwise we'd probably end up like old-fashioned sci-fi robots—all flashing lights, warning buzzers and smoke pouring from our ears as we shout 'overload'. However, this is unfortunate because we miss out on a lot of important stuff. For instance, our increasingly complex work environment, where politics and competing personalities can leave us baffled. Whatever our role, we tend to be so busy just getting along, that we rarely sit up and take notice. Those who do, have a clear edge over us.

The benefits of enhanced observation skills are plenty. To name a few, it helps in better understanding of friends and rivals, bosses and staff, it aids decision-making, helps influence people, helps you find ways to solve problems and also find opportunities. As author Jonathan Swift said, "Vision is the art of seeing things invisible to others." And why does so much of what's in front of us seem invisible? It's perhaps because, as the American philosopher, Ralph Waldo Emerson said, "people only see what they are prepared to see", or if one were to believe, English banker, John Lubbock, "what we see depends mainly on what we look for".

Frankly, making observation a habit isn't all that hard. It takes a little more than choosing a focus and, indeed, the willingness to practise. Try focussing on one event or one person at first. Be attentive at meetings, for instance, by observing behaviour and reactions. The advantages could range from anything such as communicating better with an awkward member to handling someone whom you find intimidating. So, don't keep those blinkers on. Try a little experiment with your ability to see what's going on around you. Start now. You'll be surprised to learn what keen observation can do for you.

❐

41

Small Steps, Big Help

I have always been keen on making acquaintances with an indiscernible face in the crowd, as the self-made, simple person often makes a strong impact. I remember years ago, I came across such a man, a Bubbly, self-employed, 23-year-old, who goes by the name of Nandan Pandya. This Mumbai resident doesn't possess a fat purse, but saves a paltry sum each day to buy slippers for the thousands who tread the road barefoot.

He has been doing this for the last nine months and has distributed more than 150 slippers to absolute strangers. "There are so many affluent people who make a show of their munificence, hogging the limelight for their deed. But what use are clothes and food if you can't walk that extra mile, literally, to make your daily ends meet? Walking barefoot is impossible. Couldn't I spare some money to help some of the barefoot people?" Pandya reminisced.

Stressful events beset our everyday lives. There are therapies and more therapies that experts suggest. I suggest a far simpler one – spare a few moments to help others and experience how beneficial that can be. Somebody once told me about Carolyn Schwartz, a Research Professor with the University of Massachusetts Medical School, who started a unique experiment lending an ear to patients with multiple sclerosis, doing nothing except sparing a few words of sympathy. In return for a little time invested in this, she soon started experiencing a dramatic improvement in the quality of her life, a complete takeover by a tranquil state of mind amid a chaotic milieu.

There are countless little instances we see all around us, where we can chip in to help, but often choose not to. Exceptions are awfully few, Ajmer Singh, a journalist friend, being one. While working with a Delhi newspaper years ago, he was travelling from Sundar Nagar to Dhaula Kuan by an auto-rickshaw some months ago, when he spotted the driver speaking over a fancy cell phone, which he presumed cost no less than ₹ 25,000.

A suspicious Ajmer quietly noted down the cab's registration number and rang up the nearest police station to enquire if it had any complaint regarding a lost cell phone. His suspicion came true as a businessman from Noida had indeed forgotten his gadget in an auto, never to find it again. He finally did, all due to a few moments spared by a thoughtful Ajmer Singh.

Novelist Charles Dickens said, "By helping others, you are helping yourself." So, Ajmer told me not to speak of his deed as anything heroic. Shouldn't we all follow in Ajmer's footsteps?

❐

42

Words that can Rouse a Nation

Former Pakistan President, Pervez Musharraf may not have been the best leader ever, but his words held sway over his people like no one else. I realised this on my visit to the country in 2003-04, when the Indian cricket team was to visit Pakistan five years after the disintegration of cricketing relations between the two countries.

A week before the start of the five one-day and three test matches, I visited most of the cricketing venues in Pakistan. The sojourn was an eye-opener. My being an Indian proved an impediment as no one bothered to converse with me. In fact, a Multan school kid enquired why India asked for a partition in 1947. When I asked her who told her this, she laid her claim to the knowledge on history books.

This phlegmatic milieu was to change soon. On the day of the arrival of the Indian cricket team members and onlookers, the then President of Pakistan, Parvez Musharraf, addressed the nation on television. With his trademark oratory, he dwelt on how cricket can and will iron out differences between Indians and Pakistanis and how he intended to "let us show them what Islamic hospitality is all about and that we can express love better than any Indian".

The utterances worked like magic. The next 41 days were near-blissful for me. I realised that the feeling of love and hatred can be invoked or provoked by a single catalyst like an address by a charismatic leader. Musharraf was an apotheosis of such a leader and succeeded in exhorting his countrymen into giving a warm welcome. The sea-change in the behaviour of the Pakistani public was apparent. Not only the Indian players, even spectators from across the border were accorded royal treatment.

Pakistanis offered free cold drinks, snacks and flowers. Even auto-rickshaw and cycle-rickshaw drivers declined money from the Indian passengers. When I went to shop for some Punjabi suits for my wife, along with Mandira Bedi and Murali Karthik at the Anarkali Market in Lahore, it turned out to be my best shopping experience ever, surpassing my visit to Harrods in London.

"People buy into the leader before they buy into the vision, so potent can be his words." So said American author, John C Maxwell. Such is the power of one address to the nation—one address of President Musharraf that coalesced a disparate nation into one, converting the so-called hostile behaviour into resplendent hospitality. Which then forces me to think: Are our own leaders capable of such overwhelmingly inspirational oratory?

❐

43

One Act of Kindness can Change a Life

How can I forget filmmaker Steven Spielberg's 1998 war epic *Saving Private Ryan,* where the US as a nation stood up to salute a mother who had lost three sons during World War II by tracing her last son, paratrooper James Ryan, who went missing in action somewhere in Normandy?

Back home, I was pleasantly surprised to read an article some years ago about a rarest of rare instance of employee provident fund (EPF)—with a reputation for sluggish performance—coming to the aid of a woman in Jabalpur, to assuage the anguish of her bereavement.

A news item about an unfortunate incident of electrocution claiming the lives of a school teacher, Narendra Shukla (35), and his mother (55) caught the attention of local EPF section officer, Shivendra Kamparia. Kamparia went to Shukla's house the same day where a heart-wrenching pall of grief greeted him. The bodies were about to be taken for cremation. Kamparia waited patiently until the formalities were over, introduced himself to Shukla's widow, Chetna and convinced her to fill up the form.

At this juncture, there were two hitches to speedy disposal of the PF amount. One, Chetna did not have a bank account and two, there was no death certificate. First, Kamparia got a bank account opened in Chetna's name. He then attached a newspaper clipping about Shukla's demise to it and got a cheque of the PF amount made and deposited it in Chetna's account the very next day and got an acknowledgement from Chetna.

"Just as treasures are uncovered from the earth, so virtue appears from good deeds, and wisdom appears from a pure and peaceful mind. To walk safely through the maze of human life, one needs the light of wisdom and the guidance of virtue," said Lord Buddha. To Kamparia, the deceased was a stranger, one among millions of registered EPF customers. It was one man's effort to help out someone in distress when the person needed the money urgently, is what characterises the bond that binds humanity. Shouldn't we all follow in his footsteps? For the sake of humanity.

❐

44

Make Attention to Details a Habit

Many years ago, my father suffered a failed right ventricle and had to be admitted to a hospital. When he developed complications, I called one of my colleagues and asked for the local hospital's number. I was given three seven-digit numbers. We are all aware that seven-digit numbers are now a relic and we need to prefix a '2' to the old numbers. Now that, you would say, was quite an innocuous mistake and not something to fuss over. I agree that anybody else would have glossed over it.

What I am trying to say is: Cooking at various workplaces, one gets the impression that meticulous and disciplined work is fast vanishing. If work is interpreted as worship, then worshipping has now become quite mechanical. I remember something motivational speaker and author, Gary Ryan Blair once wrote: "Discipline in work is based on meticulous attention to details, on mutual respect and confidence. Discipline must be so ingrained that it becomes a habit."

What I've learnt in a career spanning 35 years is that attention given to minute details has far-fetched results. Not only does it show your dedication to work, it's a reflection of the kind of person you are. A meticulous worker, who wouldn't expect others to take things for granted, is dependable in personal life as well. The care and concern he displays in dispensing his duties is a measure of his attitude and disposition.

Now, imagine this: If I spoke to the colleagues who gave me the seven-digit numbers, he would've retorted, "Of course, that's obvious. Can't you use your common sense? Is that something to be asked?" He would've, in fact, made me feel like an imbecile. What, in fact, would've escaped his notice is that in any profession, being accurate is important. It's required of one not to miss out even a '2'—it's a matter of professional integrity. You know, the greatest hurdle to a man's discipline at work is his ego. Even if a man were told to improve his style of functioning, he would take it as an affront. All of us, if we are honest, must have experienced this, right?

I admit that perfection is an elusive goal and is unattainable, Yes. But then, in trying to achieve it, one acquires a discipline that's so integral to the sustenance of life. So, inculcate discipline, be meticulous and win over the hearts of those around you.

❐

Bequeathal of Music for the Sake of Posterity

This happened quite a few years ago while Sitar Maestro Pandit Ravi Shankar was performing at a concert in Kolkata. A newspaper reporter asked him if Western music could ever overshadow Indian classical music. "Never," said Panditji. "One, its roots are too deep to be uprooted and two," he continued, clasping his daughter-sitarist Anoushka's hand, "there are many like us where the tradition of music is and will always be carried forward by the next generation."

The cherished Indian culture of *guru-shishya parampara* has helped good music thrive even in a generation given to a culture inspired by the West. In India, the parent-children combinations in the field of music are as varied as the music they practise. Violin exponent, N. Rajam, who is the daughter of the illustrious A. Narayana Iyer and the sister of T.N. Krishnan, has said it on record that her daughter, Sangeeta demonstrates the *gayaki* ang-style of playing the violin better than her.

"There have been so many disciples of my father, Ustad Allarakkha," renowned percussionist, Taufiq Qureshi once told me, "but what we picked up from him as part of the *guru-shishya parampara,* no one else could." Along with *tabla* maestro, Ustad Zakir Hussein and Fazal Qureshi, the trio stands out as worthy sons of a worthy father, which has carried forward the richness of the Indian musical tradition. Santoor Maestro, Pandit Shiv Kumar Sharma and Rahul, Mohan Veena exponent, Pandit Vishwa Bhatt and Salil, late vocalist, Pandit Bhimsen Joshi and Shrinivas represent but a few instances, where musical tradition has been passed on from one generation to the next.

In the same vein, I'd like to cite the example of a father-son music composer duo from Bollywood, Sachin Dev Burman and Rahul 'Pancham' Dev Burman. Sachin ruled Hindi filmdom between the 1950s and 1970s. When Pancham took over the reins from his father, people asked if he could match his father's finesse. It needn't be mentioned that Pancham took Hindi film music to a new level by fusing the best of the East and the West. The duo remains a unique example of the best of musical tradition seamlessly transferred to the next generation.

"Music is enough for a lifetime, but a lifetime isn't enough for music," goes a famous proverb. So, if you want your art to survive, you must anoint someone to take it forward. For the sake of posterity.

❐

Utterances can Soothe and Shear

There was this brief compliment from a relatively unknown person sometime in 2010 that opened my eyes as to why words are called the precursors of action – positive or negative. As a matter of routine, I was walking down the lane near my house with my dog Pixie, a cute little bundle of flesh and fur, when this gentleman, a neighbour, crossed my path accompanied by his huge Alsatian. "Know what, your little one keeps greeting me every day from your balcony, as if she wanted me to come over for a cup of coffee. Well, why don't we catch up over coffee some day? I stay in the building next to yours," said Mr. X, before disappearing with a generous smile.

I didn't get an opportunity to visit Mr. X after that, though. His name I do not know, the reason I respectfully refer to him as Mr. X. But his words left an indelible mark on my mind – a couple of utterances that formed an instant bond between two strangers. Those few words brought him so close to me that I feel as if I have known him for ages. I remember Irish playwright, George Bernard Shaw's simile on words being like postage stamps, delivering the object for you to unwrap. It being a matter of interpretation, spoken words need caution.

Years ago, my grandmother told me a story. Two children were playing on a tree when the weather got worse. The mother of the first kid screamed: "Hold the branch properly or you will fall." The second kid's mother said patiently: "Hold the branch properly, son, so that you don't fall." The first kid couldn't resist the strong wind and fell. The second held on to a branch for 45 minutes till the storm blew over. The way the mothers spoke created two distinct frames of mind. The first kid heard his mother being negative, while the second found his mother's words reassuring, which gave him strength.

Former CBI Director, Joginder Singh in one of his books says that you can't always think positively all the time, nor can you always prevent negative thoughts. But one must perpetually make an earnest attempt to keep negative thoughts at bay and watch one's mouth. Let's take heart in what former UK Prime Minister, Winston Churchill said: "By swallowing evil words unsaid, no one has ever harmed his stomach." Remember, words can bring souls together as forcefully as they can shear them apart.

❐

Truth must Prevail, but Softly

My mother once told me a story about a teacher who was discussing the picture of a student's family with the rest of the class. Innocently oblivious of tact that kids of Class I are, one of the students suggested that it seemed the boy in the picture wasn't born in the family as his hair colour was different from the rest of the family's. "Were you adopted?" he asked. The kid in question, unaware of the word, asked what adoption meant. The teacher instantly understood the trickiness of the situation and the truth that could hurt the child. She explained, "Adoption, dear, means you grew in your mommy's heart instead of her tummy!" The boy's eyes gleamed beatifically.

I recollect someone relating a similar anecdote. A Class II student from a leading school, who was physically challenged, was desperate to take part in the annual drama competition. His innocence shielded comprehensibility about his physical impediment. He kept telling his parents and teachers that he was capable of performing an act that would make them feel proud of him. Everyone was in a quandary about how to handle the situation and say 'no' to him. The class teacher kept postponing the announcement of the drama troupe till one day a novel idea struck her.

On the day the roles of the play were assigned to different students, the child's mother came to collect him after school. The boy rushed up to her, eyes shining with pride and excitement. "Guess what, Mom," he shouted, and then said those words that will remain a lesson to everyone: "I've been chosen to clap and cheer. The teacher told me that this role is as important as the rest of the cast, perhaps more, as a play is meaningless without an appreciative audience." There were tears in his mother's eyes. She understood.

"The truth is the sole way to the soul's salvation," goes a proverb. Notwithstanding the truth's power to enlighten and emancipate, it is, perhaps, the most difficult pronouncement for the human tongue to make. It's bitter. It stings, singes. It's almost like a whip that strips you naked to the bone. As George Eliot had said, it is hard to say the exact truth and harder still to say something fine which is not the exact truth. No wonder that we all believe that when it comes to children – possessors of impressionable minds – we should take it easy. You may not be able to sugarcoat the truth, but you could put it in a manner that makes truth a salve instead of a stick.

❐

48

Make Your Child Your Friend

An interview of Amin Sayani brought back decades-old memories of *Binaca Geet Mala* on Radio Ceylon, when, as a student, I sat behind closed doors with the volume of my small transistor turned low, as the presenter played the golden melodies. I was afraid, actually dead frightened, of my father, who didn't quite relish the idea of his son riding the musical cadences. Those were times when the father – the patriarch of the family - spelt terror and whose wishes were destiny. Fear forbade me to even speak to him, let alone demand the fulfilment of a wish.

Fast forward to the present times. I remember my daughter called me saying her mother had reneged on her promise to take her out for dinner. "Not to worry, dear," I comforted her, "Cheer up. I'll accompany you for dinner."

The parent-child relationship has undergone a paradigm shift. The question-me-not attitude has melted, the distance has narrowed and what were previously called taboo subjects are now discussed like friends would. Yes, as 'friends'. Times have changed, and so have the parameters of relationships. To be frank, I enjoyed taking my daughter out. It helps me extend a hand of friendship, which my father couldn't.

A parent-child relationship doesn't occur in a vacuum, and the context in which it develops is likely to affect the nature of it. Marc Bornstein's *Handbook of Parenting* says that factors such as birth order, financial and emotional stress, parent gender, infant temperament and parent personality may influence the relationship and impact the child's development. When I refer to my daughter as 'friend', I do not mean to trivialize the relationship. I am merely trying to accentuate the need for a more pragmatic approach to help build a healthier relationship, whereby, a parent becomes a rudder for the child. To this end, little gestures like saying 'I love you' can work wonders.

"How pleasant it is for a father to sit at his child's board. It is like an aged man reclining under the shadow of an oak which he has planted," said French writer, Voltaire. Spending quality time can infuse more life into the relationship. Offering space to accommodate a child's points of view will cement the bond. Above all, let's remember that faith is the cornerstone of all relationships. So, make an effort to promote the milieu of glasnost, of candour and openness, where misgivings are discussed, not repressed. When we are talking of children, we are talking of minds, that too impressionable ones. One wrong stroke can mar, while patience and continued guidance can make a life.

❐

Do It Yourself, Discover

The narrow lane in Nagpur, where I lived during my childhood, will forever remain a part of me. I used to distribute *Nagpur Times* or *Hitwada* to all the 40-45 houses by 6.30 am, without fail. "One complaint and you lose 20 *paise*," the vendor would tell me. That was in 1975, and as a student of standard X, I doubled up as a newspaper vendor to earn my own pocket money. The work wasn't easy. I was faced with placating people with varied mood swings. One grumpy octogenarian wouldn't have his newspaper delivered a minute after 6 am. Another would change his newspaper almost every second day. A retired armyman would never admit that I delivered the newspaper all 30 days.

Thanks to my parents who taught me on to earn my own pocket money, which was some ₹ 60 then. I did that job for six months before I settled to prepare for my SSC exam. More than 40 years on, when I look back, I remember my father's words, "No work is big or small, my son. It's not the stature of work that matters, but what you learn from working that counts. Never listen to people who tell you that the work you are doing is demeaning or would undermine your prestige. Remember, work doesn't undermine prestige, it is the absence of work that does."

My father, a class 1 railway official, could have given me all the pocket money I wanted. My sister and I could have had all the fun the moment we pressed the request button. However, my father thought differently. The '70s was a time when things were easy-going. But my father saw tough times germinating somewhere in the near future. He knew that by the time I was ready to take on the mantle, things would be hard, very hard. So, the more self-dependent he made me, the more would I be able to reap the harvest of happiness.

"Twenty years from now, you will be more disappointed by the things that you didn't do than by the ones you did do. So, throw off the bowlines. Sail away from the safe harbour. Catch the trade winds in your sails. Explore. Dream. Discover," said American author, Mark Twain. Every job prepares us to confront unforeseen adversities. Left to fend for oneself early in life, one learns the ropes and gets tougher with time. Brought up in a shielded atmosphere, one may find life's rigmarole too dazzling to handle. Remember the adage: When the going gets tough, only the tough get going.

❐

A Customer is also a Father

Do you remember actor Anupam Kher's spirited performance in the movie *Saaransh,* in which he plays a father shattered by his son's untimely death? In the movie, Kher's character confronts a government official, who asks him to wait his turn among those waiting for goodies from abroad and pleads with him that all he wants are his son's ashes.

I know of one M.S. Shrivastava, a retired employee of State Bank of India (SBI) in Ujjain, who faced a similar predicament. He wanted his son's Sony Ericsson mobile's battery replaced after seven years of its purchase. For him the handset was the last reminder of his loved one, whom he lost in an unfortunate accident. Shrivastava had two daughters and one son. In June 2003, his daughter gifted a mobile handset to her younger brother. Meanwhile, Shrivastava's elder daughter, who after marriage had moved to Surat, invited them home in July 2004. Shrivastava's brother's son was also roped in for the trip.

The four along with the son-in-law went to Suwali Beach near Surat for a picnic. Unfortunately, the four drowned, and the son-in-law was saved by the rescue helicopter. A shattered Shrivastava came back home with the mobile phone. Whenever the phone rang, he felt as if his children were calling. Since then Shrivastava senior started using the mobile. However, after a while, the battery needed replacement and he began to scout for one.

Since the company had stopped the production of that model, the battery wasn't available. But Shrivastava didn't want to discard the mobile for emotional reasons. He contacted the company's service centre, but couldn't get one. He didn't lose heart.

Finally, he made one last attempt and sent an email to the firm's president, Bert Nordberg in the US. The email narrated a heart-rending story of that 'sacred relation' with his children, who were no more. A few days later, he was informed by the head of Indian operations and also the customer relations department that the company was searching for the availability of the battery globally and would revert soon. A week later, he was informed that it was available in Singapore. A few days later, the battery was couriered to his residential address. After his mail to the firm's president, he received a replacement in exactly 22 days.

How many other global companies know how to value their customers and their emotions? "Submission is not about authority and it is not obedience; it is all about relationships of love and respect," said Canadian author, W. Paul Young. Are companies out there listening?

❐

51

Teach Tramps to Perform

During my visits to Bangalore, I stay at a guest house on Lavelle Road opposite the Majestic Cubbon Park and I make it a point not to miss a rendezvous with the park's musical Sundays. Right in the centre of the gorgeous open space, a bunch of performers line up to play their hearts out every Sunday morning starting at 6. The show lasts almost two hours, after which a mix of the cybercity's joggers cheer(s) them, their claps reverberating through the serene ambience of the green space.

But each time, before the audience can come out of the musical trance, they are intercepted by a gaggle of beggars and tramps beseeching them for alms. That, my friends, is like the fly in the ointment for all visitors to Cubbon Park. The untimely interception often makes me wonder if it is possible to gainfully employ mendicants and help them earn a livelihood.

In Mumbai, near the airport, vagrants are not allowed to beg and if someone breaches this rule, he is at the mercy of a police constable's cane. Why can't we identify such drifters, train them on the basis of their strengths and make them street performers? Heritage experts and town planners the world over have been successful in training homeless individuals in busking or street performance. This is especially true in cities that have many heritage monuments.

The practice of busking—performing in public precincts for meagre tips—can also restore their dignity. Busking acts can be anything that tourists find entertaining.

They can be trained in theatre, gymnastics, animal performances, card tricks, clowning, mime, dance, juggling and magic tricks. Other art forms like musical performances, puppeteering, snake charming, storytelling, poetry recitals, sketching and painting could be sponsored by corporate groups. Near the Charles Bridge in Prague or near the Eiffel Tower in Paris, the imaginative use of common instruments has been deployed to telling effect. A simple i-Pod attached to an amplifier, on which the performer can play a single musical instrument, can give the audience an impression of orchestra-jamming.

In the US, buskers can be spotted at various locations frequented by travellers and tourists. Subway stations and gardens like the Central Park are their favourite haunts. "Children are great imitators. So, give them something to imitate," says an ancient Chinese proverb. India's IT hub, Bangalore can take this up as a case study and introduce street performers, most of whom are children, to a new livelihood, and more essentially, self-respect. If not all over Bangalore, the experiment can be tried out at least at Cubbon Park and Lalbagh.

❒

52

Think Big to Achieve

My teenage daughter, a die-hard fan of martial arts movies, once forced me to watch the 1978 Hollywood flick *36th Chamber of Shaolin*. Though not enormously enamoured of such violent flinging of the arms and legs, one particular scene in the movie moved me. The protagonist—played by Gordon Liu—a new recruit at the Shaolin temple, practises all night to master the art of kung fu while the world sleeps. Soon, he outdoes his colleagues and emerges triumphant. It made me think of the athlete Milkha Singh.

"What if I told you Milkha Singh was an expert cook before he became an ace sportsman?" I asked my daughter the next day. She looked flummoxed. I told her how by sheer tenacity of purpose, Milkha Singh 'the cook' became one of India's greatest athletes earning the sobriquet of 'Flying Sikh'.

Milkha's is one of the countless faces that bears ineradicable scars of the Partition. Born in Lyallpur (Pakistan), having lost his parents to the Partition, he hid behind corpses in the train that was carrying his family to India. He began as a cook in the army. But his mind was never on making porridge and stew for the jawans' breakfast. He watched them jogging in the morning and said to himself, "But I can run faster and have more stamina than them. Why can't I run?" Then, he hit upon the idea of practising running in the night when everyone slept. He dreaded being spotted. So, his nocturnal sessions became shorter, his speed faster. Until one day, he was caught. "A fast-running cook, eh?" the major derided. "OK, you run with my boys tomorrow morning."

Army superiors watched with dropped jaws the next morning as Milkha completed his round when trained jawans were less than half-way to the target. It was as if there were wheels attached to his feet. His talent was spotted, honed and chiselled, until a perfect athlete emerged. The rest is history. Though he lost the bronze by a heart-breaking 0.1 second in the 400 m race behind Malcolm Spence of South Africa in the 1960 Olympics, national titles flowed one after the other.

I am reminded of what American billionaire, Donald Trump said, "As long as you think, think big." That's one of the secrets of success. Think big and you are bound to reach there in pursuance of your goal.

❐

53

Speak Less, Listen

A trainee journalist walked up to me and asked me about his progress. "You have done a fabulous job so far," I said, "but you'll have to work harder." "Harder?" he almost yelled, "I am already working very hard. I come early in the morning and stay till late in the night, I re-write at least seven stories and design two pages...."

He went on and on, and I could see he was dejected by my comment. I asked him to sit down and tried to explain he ought to focus more on his editing skills. But he never let me. Evidently, he wasn't a good listener.

Note that I wasn't complaining, but the young gentleman read it like that. While I was exhorting a member of my team to work in a certain way, he extinguished all possibilities of appreciating the real message, reacting to his own assumed meaning.

Listening is a virtue few possess. Most of us are 'already always listening'. Simply put, this means we assume what is being said to us. Instead of listening with attention, we focus our mental energies on responding to what is being said. Listening is an essential part of communication. Being a good and patient listener helps you not only to solve many problems at work and home, but helps you see the world through the eyes of others. It thereby opens your understanding and enhances your capacity to empathize.

You learn a lot by just listening. Of course, it takes sincere effort and lots of practice but listening makes people feel special. They feel worthy, appreciated and respected. Wouldn't we all want that? Studies prove that listening is a skill we can learn to cultivate. Remember, listening to our kids helps build their self-esteem and the parent-child bond. It is something every parent craves for. Most of us blabber because our gargantuan egos come in our way. "I must be heard, not he," is what plays on our psyche. But try listening and you will see that you will be able to speak better, and the world will be your oyster.

As American author and entrepreneur, Brian Koslow said, "If one spends more time listening and asking questions than giving answers or opinions, he is bound to taste success." Success involves learning and one can learn more if he gives his tongue some rest.

❐

54

Respond, Don't React

Years ago, as a kid mortally afraid of mathematics, I remember being smacked across my face by my mother the moment I came home after a bad paper. Since mathematics was the first exam and would almost inevitably go wrong, my mother's reaction to my saying that I fared badly would be a shrill cry followed by a flurry of slaps and disparaging comments. In sheer disgust, I would not be able to concentrate on other subjects, the exams of which followed on subsequent days. I am sure most of us share this childhood experience. Had my mother controlled her reaction and responded in a more mellowed manner, my scores in subjects other than mathematics could have climbed many notches higher.

The point I am trying to make is: 'Respond, don't react'. There is a huge difference between reacting and responding. A reaction is a thoughtless, emotional impulse resulting in a negative view. Contrarily, a response involves thought, and, shorn of emotions, projects a positive perspective. The listener finds it soothing and it might just make his day, maybe yours too.

Let alone a child, a reaction could have serious implications for a grown-up. I remember Joel Schumacher's film, *Falling Down*, where actor, Michael Douglas, who plays an ordinary man, reacts to minor day-to-day provocations by picking up a gun to settle scores. In the end, he is shot by a cop. We face many hurdles in life whose answers lie not in violent reaction, but in tackling them with cool responsiveness, lest we 'fall' like Douglas in the film.

"Life is 10% what happens to you and 90% how you react to it," said author and educator, Charles R. Swindoll. Sometimes, we have to make a split decision whether to react or respond. Our natural instinct is to react. A natural proclivity towards responding, however, comes with time and practice. Try it. You have all to gain.

❒

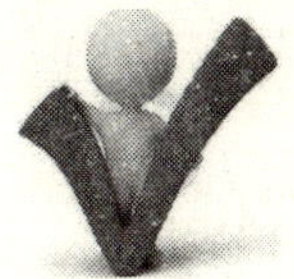

55

Call of Power from Within

It's great to have a good body. After all, physical attributes make the first impression. But you can't disagree that beyond the visible roaring biceps and the six-pack abs, lies the true force of human life – inner strength.

It is this strength that's real and supersedes the external brawns. It is what helps you achieve, lies in believing that you are all-powerful. The day you believe so, the word 'fear' will be effaced from the lexicon of your life. An incident related by Swami Vivekananda in his autobiography comes to my mind. While on a trip to Benares, he was pursued by a troop of monkeys. Vivekananda ran and was almost out of breath, when an elderly ascetic cried out to him, "Don't run. Face the brutes!"

Drawing on his inner strength, Vivekananda turned around, fearlessly. The monkeys were jolted by his sudden defiance and backed out. Years later in New York, in one of his lectures, Vivekananda, quoting this incident, said, "That's a lesson for life. Face the terrible, face it boldly. Like the monkeys, the hardships of life dissipate when we cease to flee from them."

The 'brute' in all of us is the underlying fear of the unknown. The essence of life is not in winning over the inevitable, but in fighting it to the end. It's then that you have lived life to the brim. I remember watching 'Farrah's

Story', a sometimes uplifting, sometimes painful documentary that chronicles American actress, Farrah Fawcett's fight against cancer on NBC. A multiple Golden Globe and Emmy Award nominee, Fawcett rose to international fame when she first appeared as private investigator, Jill Munroe in the TV series, *Charlie's Angels* in 1976. Billed as Hollywood's sex symbol in the 1970s and 1980s, Farrah's placid and bountiful life came apart when she was diagnosed with cancer in 2006. She could have reacted in two ways. She could've either resigned to the situation, or could've fought the inevitable. Farrah chose the second option.

She gathered all her inner strength and soldiered on. A heart-warming moment in the documentary comes when in the end, Farrah asks the audience, "I have fought my battle. Tell me, what are you fighting for?"

In September 2009, Farrah passed away. You would say she lost out to cancer, but I say she was a winner even in death. Today, Farrah lives on through her tale of grit and zest for life in the face of odds.

The message is: Face the brute (read fear) even if you know you are going to be killed. Fight till you are killed. Don't die of fright, die fighting.

❐

56

A Thought for All

When Anil Mudgal, who runs Arushi, an NGO in Bhopal, first showed me a railway reservation requisition slip for West Central Railway, I was a tad flummoxed as I couldn't spot anything outstanding. The form had instructions printed in English and Hindi on one side and titbits on Braille on the flip side.

Strange, I thought. Until he explained, that is. "How many times have you misjudged a person just because he hasn't returned your pleasantries?" Anil asked me. "Well, there is no question of an erroneous judgement if I know the person in question. If I know him well, I usually infer that he might be too perturbed to return my greetings," I countered. "That's precisely it. You know the person too well to form an instant opinion. Most of us are obstinately opinionated, because more often than not, we do not know someone and are hence unable to appreciate his feelings," Mudgal said.

Linking this to the rationale behind printing information about Braille on the reservation slip, an endeavour successfully initiated by Arushi, he said that awareness was the key to better understanding and appreciation of a special condition. He thought of sensitising people about the blind through the railways. The West Central Railway previously had forms printed in English and Hindi on either side. Arushi officials impressed upon the railway authorities the futility of printing the form in two languages on both sides. Why not print both on the same side to save printing costs, they argued.

As the logic gained acceptance, Arushi got the other side of the form printed with information on the Braille script. Their reasoning was simple. Fiddling with the form while standing in the queue, even if some people turned it over and read the nuggets on how those less fortunate make an effort to try and be one of us, they would know how to deal with them. Most passengers take two forms, hand over one at the ticket counter and take the other home. If some of them care to read about Braille later or tell others about it, the purpose is doubly served, Arushi officials reasoned.

A small beginning, yes, but it serves a greater purpose. Not a question of the blind alone, it is more a matter of giving due regard to every fellow human being. The thin line demarcating civility and barbarity is governed by the art of understanding people. "I am only one, but I am one. I cannot do everything, but I can do something. And I will not let what I cannot do with what I can do," said American author, Edward Everett Hale. Believe me, a little can make a lot of difference.

❐

57

Judicious Decision

My mind goes back to the day, sometime in 2010 I think, when I entered my house after a short trip to Tirupathi, an assortment of commodities lying on the sofa caught my attention: 24 small Re 1 Parle-G biscuit packets, a plastic tiffin box and a pencil box containing 10 pencils with an eraser and a sharpener.

I was a tad surprised, what with no kids in the household. "The Sahib in flat no. A-702 gave them to me and said they were a present," my maid informed me. Why the present, she couldn't say.

The following day, I caught up with the 'sahib of flat no. A-702', one Yashdev Bahl, in the course of my morning walk. Pleasantries done, I couldn't stop asking him about the present. "Oh, that," gushed the near-octogenarian, "well, you see, it was my brother, Indra Dev's 82nd birth anniversary and I intended to give some gifts to all the 145 servants and workers of the society in his memory."

Touching gesture, I thought, but why the unusual conglomerate? What the retired electrical engineer explained, I'll never forget. Bahl said that his father passed away in 1948 when he was three years old and it was his brother who took charge of the family. "I always wanted to keep his memory alive by doing this tiny bit for the less privileged," Bahl said. But how – gift money, eatables? All that would be transient, he concluded. A gift, he inferred, should look beyond immediate needs. "Instead of a large packet, if biscuits were given in small wrappers, they would be consumed slowly and thus last longer. As for pencils, many schools offer books for free, but not writing materials. So, I thought a pack of 10 pencils would last at least three months. The tiffin box, you ask? Think, food is cooked in every household, howsoever poor, but there aren't utensils to carry it to school. My small effort will at least enable some kids to enjoy their school break."

Well-thought out acts of kindness are really not that difficult. An intention is formed and you carry it out. It makes everyone feel good. Holding kindness and compassion in our heart and integrating them into the complexity and stresses of daily life—that's the challenge. Allowing the spirit of kindness to permeate our collective lives would be a quantum leap from an evolutionary standpoint.

"Kindness is the golden chain by which society is bound together," said German writer, Goethe. Bahl believes his is only a small gesture, but says if everybody made this kind of effort within his capacity, the world would be a much better place to live in.

❐

58

Learn to Coexist

On July 26, 2005, Mumbai was inundated with 944 mm of rainfall. A lady near the airport at Kalina saw passengers scrambling on the upper deck of a stranded BEST bus. She could have opted to shut her eyes, and door.

Instead, that midnight, she used all her *saris* to create a tightrope for the passengers between her balcony and the bus, and gave them shelter until the water subsided the following morning. What's striking in this tale is that she knew all humans in this world have to share a common place somewhere. It always helps to extend a helping hand during a crisis. And amicable coexistence makes the world a happier place.

By the same logic, humans and animals occupy a hemisphere where both are dependent on the other for ecology to nurture the cycle of life. How many of us spare a thought for their troubles? Consider the monsoons, for instance. When I see animals and birds without a home, ravaged by rains, I am touched.

Before the onset of the monsoon every year, I build a little canopy with a plastic sheet at one corner of my window box-grille allowing stray cats to seek shelter. At the opposite farthest end, I keep a little bird's nest for some frightened winged ones to find temporary refuge. Even within our housing complex, birds' nests are kept on the tree branches which offer shelter during the monsoon months, until the month of September.

But are we doing anything exemplary? None, whatsoever. It's simply our way of acknowledging that ecologically it is an existential imperative that we respect animals and birds who are part of our collective life-system. It's during a crisis that we assure our fellow beings that we are alongside them.

Remember what English writer, George Bernard Shaw said, "The worse(t) sin towards our fellow creatures is not to hate them, but to be indifferent to them. That's the essence of inhumanity." For our own good, we can't do without them.

❐

59

Help Postman Survive

"And none will hear the postman's knock. Without a quickening of the heart, for who can bear to feel himself forgotten?" Somebody read out these lines from W.H. Auden's poem, *Night Mail* to me. I had almost forgotten the poem... and postmen, too. My mind, on hearing these lines from the wonderful poem I'd read years ago, went back to the times when, as a boy hardly stepping into my fifth year, I watched my grandma serving *chhaas* (butter-milk) to Ravindran, the local postman in Kumbakonam near Thanjavur.

Well into his 50s, having carried a hefty bag on his shoulders for 30 long years, Ravindran's drooping shoulders told a story of the onerous rigmarole he'd been through. He was a favourite among all the homes in our locality. Not only was he a deliverer of missives, he was also someone people looked forward to deliver money orders and small gifts wrapped in glossy papers sent by relatives.

The concept of a postman is waning in posh metros. But there are exceptions. Postmen still rule places, and indeed hearts, amid the pall of modernity. Even today in Dharavi's slums, it's not couriers that regularly do the rounds, but the dear old postman. The old charm is still retained, as people expectantly wait for him to deliver those diminutive postcards, inland letters, yellow envelopes and, of course, money orders with little amounts, which bring in a whole world of joy.

You know what? Postmen operating amid all the advancement and technology reinforce the faith, that tradition or roots can never be effaced by time's tide. I remember my uncle sending me ₹ 20 (a king's amount then) on my birthday from Mumbai every year. As the D-day approached, I would wait with bated breath for Ravindran. The joy of receiving that money order is something I haven't experienced ever again.

Our postman, Ravindran also read out letters to the unlettered and chipped in with nuggets of advice whenever required. Do you find that often? You still would, if you were to go to remote pockets, where postmen are regarded with respect. I believe that tradition should never be forsaken. Even today when I need to send money to my cousins in my village, I prefer the postal service. When I receive the little postcards from my aunt, who lives near Bangalore, my *joie de vivre* knows no bounds.

As an old saying goes, "A letter is an unannounced visit, the *postman* the agent of surprises." Trust me, tradition gives joy like none else. Bolster it, help postman survive.

❒

60

True to Your Calling

As I sat savouring Rajkumar Hirani's film *Three Idiots* in 2010, a deluge of thoughts flooded my mind. Loosely based on author, Chetan Bhagat's bestseller *Five Point Someone*, the film can be interpreted as a heart-felt portrayal of reality. It traces the lives of engineering students forced into their field by extraneous pressures while their heart's calling lies somewhere else.

What I found to be particularly interesting was the overwhelming reaction of young viewers – who formed a major chunk of the audience – to the basic premise that the film hinges on. There's a stage in everyone's life when they have to decide what they intend to do with their lives. The choice, once made, decides the course of their future. Unfortunately, we are often not able to pursue what we really want to. Our own aspirations and interests are overweighed by those of our parents, teachers, peers and, indeed, the world, which merry-go-rounds on a pursuit of fame and lucre. The question that is relegated to the backburner is: What is the kind of work that will give us real satisfaction?

I am reminded of author Hervey Taylor's statement, "I live to think for myself. I refuse to be a mindless sheep following the crowd into cookie-cutter oblivion." Now, that's a tough decision to make. Worldly pressures are too strong. The accent is on power and pelf and the film poignantly asks the question: You may amass power and pelf but do you cease to be a human who answers his heart's desire in the bargain?

You, the young at the crossroads of making the most momentous decision of your life, are all-important. Your time is limited, don't waste it living someone else's life. Don't be trapped by dogma, which is living the result of other people's thinking. Don't let the noise of somebody else's opinion drown your inner voice. And most important, have the courage to follow your heart and intuition, they somehow already know what you truly want to become.

Whenever you are stuck with indecision, answer a simple question: Will I be happy making a decision for myself following my heart's desire or should I let someone else do it for me and rue it for the rest of my life? Remember, there is no back gear in life. Steps once taken can't be retraced. For courage, take heart in Robert Frost's poem "The Road Not Taken":

"I took the road less travelled by,
And that has made all the difference."

❒

61

Train Your Mind

Consider these two instances. My friend's son, who successfully cleared the bank probationary exams some years ago, was asked two questions in course of the viva-voce. One of the interviewers asked him: "Tell me, Mr. Ravindran, what if I decide to run away with your sister?" The 24-year-old thought for a while before replying: "Great, Sir. I couldn't find a better husband for my sister." Placing a cup of coffee before him, another interviewer said: "This is the last question of this interview. Please point out the exact position of the centre of this table." Ravindran confidently put one of his fingers at some point on the table and said it was the centre. The interviewer asked how he knew that for sure. Ravindran was quick to reply: "Sir, you said this was the last question. So, I took a wild guess to a wild question."

Ravindran was selected with an excellent score. The two answers Ravindran gave do not sound awfully innovative *per se*. However, what's striking is the fact that he succeeded in giving replies that weren't stereotyped. In short, Ravindran's replies were out-of-the-box responses, which defied a rigid mindset. Moreover, it's difficult to think differently when faced with an off-the-cuff question. There are certain set patterns to the way humans react. Those who can think in split seconds and react in an unconventional manner are considered to be capable of coping with uncalled for troubles. This is no child's play and requires utmost mental equanimity. And that, you would agree, is exactly what recruiters look for in any field of work.

In any given circumstance, a question pertaining to running away with one's sister would be construed as provocative. Ravindran, however, kept his cool and turned the tables on the interviewer. In the second instance, he took advantage of the question being the last and went one-up on the interviewer.

"I don't wait for moods. You accomplish nothing if you do that. Your mind must know it has got to get down to work," said author, *Pearl S. Buck.* In a *fiercely* competitive world, where every inch of conceivable space on the mind web is occupied by innovative ideas, commonplace reactions are unwelcome. To think differently is not all that difficult. All one needs to do is train the mind to maintain calm when the wind gets wild. Out-of-the-box thinking is arduous but often rewarding as it proves that the person knows his stuff. Of course, the process involves boxing around with a lot of ideas to finally come up with a knock-out punch.

❐

62

Success Needs Sweat and More

In course of one of the long-winding discussions with my daughter on how hard work unfailingly yields fruits, she asked, "But not everyone can be a Dhirubhai Ambani, right Dad?" "One needn't be," was my riposte. "But one can certainly be Surjan Singh Ahuja," I said. "Surjan? Who?" my daughter queried. I told her, and I'll tell you now.

The humility in the smile behind the bushy beard was infectious as the fifty-something Sardar clasped my hand. It must have been the late '80s. The place: Kalbadevi in Mumbai. "Meet Surjan Singh Ahuja, owner of the biggest cloth shop in the area," a journalist friend did the formalities. "I'm a small man, Sir. Worked hard to reach here," the self-effacing man told me.

The flames of partition were yet to be doused when Surjan reached Mumbai in 1947. As a refugee in Kalbadevi, he got a menial job with a cloth shop and a shelter at a Dickensian slum nearby. Vivacious at 15, he befriended many Gujarati cloth merchants there. In between his slog, he would often visit the Kalbadevi Gurdwara, only to be stung by the sight of poor Punjabi women without *chunnis* to cover their heads inside the sanctum. An aghast Surjan struck a deal with his Gujarati friends. He would buy cloth from them, make *chunnis* and sell them to poor women at the Gurdwara for 3-4 *annas*. His profit: an *anna* a *chunni*.

Soon, he would work in the shop in the morning, sell *chunnis* at the Gurdwara at noon and go from house to house in the evening, selling his wares to families. "I wanted to help the poor Punjabi women. Profit was secondary," I remember Surjan telling me. Gradually, his earnings rose. From *chunnis* to shirt, trouser and suit cut-pieces—his business ramified, clientele burgeoned. The growing years saw him being rechristened from Surjan Singh *dupattawala* to Surjan Singh cloth merchant. Now, he had the biggest cloth showroom in Kalbadevi.

More than twenty years after our meeting, Surjan, owner of Ahuja Silk Mills in Kurla, became one of the richest Sikhs in Mumbai. What's striking in this instance of 'Singh is King' is not merely an affirmation of American inventor, Thomas Alva Edison's 'Success-is-99%-perspiration theory', but also the fact that philanthropy needn't part with fame. Surjan donates generously to Guru Nanak Hospital and educational trust, while his sons manage his business. Verily, hard work, bolstered by gumption and a touch of humanity, can never ever fail anyone.

Success is a journey, not a destination. The doing is usually more important than the outcome.

❐

Each Individual is Important

Each time I come to Pune, I learn something new from this city. Take, for instance, two Pune-based NGOs who have come together to push for the cause of Braille menu cards in restaurants. The move is aimed at ensuring that visually-challenged customers do not have to depend on others while choosing something as simple as what they want to eat at a restaurant.

Two popular restaurants of Pune—Vaishali on Fergusson College Road and Hotel Woodland at Sadhu Vaswani Chowk—have already got their menu cards transcribed in Braille.

Visually-challenged people often feel embarrassed to go to the restaurants only because they have to depend on others to read out the menu. Moreover, with some visually-challenged people conducting business meetings in restaurants over lunch, it became important to cater to their needs when it came to menu cards for hotels.

The menu cards of both the restaurants were sourced and reformatted to remove pictures and rearrange them in a suitable manner. "After deleting the unnecessary parts and editing the menu, the entire list was transcribed into

Braille. The different pages were bound together by the visually-challenged children of the NGOs."

Earlier, the waiter or one of the attendants had to read out the menu to a visually-challenged customer. But now, they can take their own time to decide what they want to eat and read the menu themselves, which makes them proud of being able to take their own decision.

Pune being an education hub like Kota and with a sizable number of visually-challenged people pursuing their degree and post-graduate courses, it becomes sensible for Pune restaurants to try out this new methodology. And indeed, they are giving these people the respect they deserve. Didn't American baseball player, Jackie Robinson say, "I'm not concerned with your liking or disliking me.... All I ask is that you respect me as a human being."

There is a lesson here to be learnt. It's about creating the feeling for everybody that they are equally important for the mainstream society. This is now a social cause espoused by many business houses. This will certainly make everybody proud and employees take a pride of serving those people who are neglected all along.

❐

64

From Dad, with Love

Growing up on ideals is common, but living an example isn't. Brinda Venkataramanan had an example in her father, P. Muthuswamy, which she knew was tough to emulate.

Rewind to the 1930s. The sincerity with which Muthuswamy acquired education—riding on his father's shoulders as the latter swam across two canals to reach the school 4 km away—was exemplary. Cut to May 2000. Muthuswamy passed away after making a success of his company, Swamy Publishers, with an unfulfilled dream: that of building a high school for poor students. Brinda decided to give him a present on June 22, his birthday and a day after Father's Day. She succeeded.

Five years before his death, Muthuswamy bought a small plot in Porur, 40 km from Chennai, with a view to starting a school for underprivileged children. A diminutive building came up housing classes KG to V. Admissions were strictly restricted to those who lived within a four-km radius of the school, the distance he travelled on his father's shoulders. With Muthuswamy's death, Brinda took it upon herself to fulfil her father's dream of making it a high school. She built another building to accommodate classes VI to XII, and there was no turning back.

"The 100 per cent results in the classes X and XII state examinations don't please me. The real pleasure is in seeing a grocer's daughter making it to medical school or a florist's son getting into IIT. My father's unfulfilled dreams find fruition in each of these children," Brinda told me. "My school may not be well-known in Tamil Nadu, but then I don't cater to page three socialites. I serve vendors, maids and menial job-doers, who dream of their children becoming 'somebody'," she said. She is currently constructing another building for pre-primary kids. "Don't you think my father would have been pleased with my gift?" Brinda asks me.

"He didn't tell me how to live; he lived and let me watch him do it," said the 19th century American writer, Clarence Budington Kelland about his father. Undoubtedly. Humble roots nourished by lofty values of discipline, quality and relentless pursuit of perfection—these are what Brinda learnt from her father in the school of life. And she gave them back to him by building on his unfulfilled dreams. Don't we all have something to learn from Brinda Venkataramanan?

❒

Try to Avoid Human Errors

I was once part of a survey which undertook a research on why robberies often happen in some cooperative societies, while no such robberies are recorded in other societies. The findings were strange. The society in which the security guards kept saluting the members when they make an exit or entry never registered a case of robbery while the society where the security guards were selective in saluting certain members (like committee members of the society) has registered robbery cases.

This made the findings look strange. But here are facts: When a security guy salutes and says either good morning or good afternoon or good night, he engages the muscles of the mouth and arm, which indirectly stimulates the brain to keep him alert.

In Japan, the train drivers are asked to do this. While approaching every signal, the driver of a train would raise his hand and point at the signal ahead, whether red or green, and would say the colour loudly. He would register the colour of the signal with a word to himself and stab at the signal again with his finger for emphasis. This is like a mono act play from the driver's cabin. By doing this, the driver makes sure that he does not get the signal wrong. This method is called *Shisa Kanko* in Japanese. This effort has reduced the human error in accidents to one per-cent from three per-cent.

I always used this method since I read this piece in *The Japan Times* in 1985, while operating my bank locker. After operating the bank locker and making an exit, a suspicion ran through my mind, "Did I keep all ornaments back in locker?" or "Did I close the locker properly?" To avoid such stupid questions to come back in brain, I would always say to myself that I had closed the locker and kept everything back in the locker loudly as there is no one in the locker room, except for the locker owner. Similarly, many of us have the habit that after leaving home for a family function, we suddenly get edgy about whether we have closed the taps properly or whether we have switched off the lights and fans.

"It's human to make errors, but human still to be cautious to try not to make them," said former UK Prime Minister, Winston Churchill. Elementary things can be practised and implemented to avoid accidents that occur due to human sloppiness. And they should not be considered below dignity.

❐

66

The Beauty Within

I remember having read an article in the early 1980s about a woman from north India, whose grit paved the way for many oppressed women to follow suit. Wife of a bureaucrat, she was an exquisitely beautiful woman with a heart of gold. Everyone, right from children in the neighbourhood to the municipal sweeper, admired her nature—kind, affable and patient. But there was trouble on the home front. Her husband, given to drinking and promiscuity, wanted to 'use' his wife's physical charm to further his own career. One evening, after a nasty altercation with her, the husband took a bottle of concentrated acid and threw it on her face. The right side of her face, including the facial bones, almost melted away. A plastic surgery followed, whereby, a metal plate was used to hold up one side of her face. The once-beautiful woman now looked grotesque.

Beyond the veneer of appearance, her heart, however, grew more beautiful. A divorce later, she lent her entire life to help countless such battered women from various states seek justice. Her outward beauty was ruined, which only made her inner goodness stronger. It is this inner beauty that the likes of her foster and which humanity must salute.

Decades ago, my moral science teacher said something I remember to this day: "You don't love a woman because she's beautiful. She is beautiful because you love her. Look for beauty within, not without. Go for the Mona Lisa heart, not the smile." The message didn't strike me as potently then as it did after I heard this woman's story. It pains me today to see how we are often swept off our feet by outward gloss and affectation, scarcely concerned with the glow of goodness that emanates from within.

The problem is that the concept of beauty has been commercialised. Beauty is not confined to looks alone. It can come in the form of nature, of people's souls, of art and words, and more. The concept of beauty is strictly individual—you can either choose to be lulled by what looks beautiful, or choose to be charmed by the pristine inner beauty of the human heart.

Many of us, including myself, often look at outside beauty. But it's only when you know someone and see who they are that you begin to realise that real beauty radiates from the inside. As Kahlil Gibran said, "Beauty is not in the face, beauty is a light in the heart."

❐

SECTION-IV

You are Supreme. Give Yourself a Chance

67

Looks are Deceptive

I was once returning from Nagpur to Sevagram. The train left early morning. Normally, I used to introduce myself right away to the person sitting next to me, but on this particular occasion, I just didn't feel like it. The man sitting next to me was in his mid-20s with blood-shot eyes. He reeked of cheap after-shave and wore a loud jacket that seemed to have been the fashion of those days. I glanced at him without enthusiasm, holding my backpack without putting it on the luggage rack overhead as if this ruffian would run away with.

He, however, was inclined to be in a chatty mood. He attempted to strike a conversation again and again. I replied in short staccato sentences, making my annoyance evident. Finally, he got the message and lapsed into a sullen silence. It was time to catch some sleep. Deeply distrustful of the man's intentions, I curled myself into a tiny ball, trying to squeeze myself well within the boundary of my own seat. It was cold outside, and my window wouldn't close completely. The cool breeze soon lulled me into sleep despite my wariness.

Suddenly, I woke up with a start due to a commotion. I found, to my horror, that the seat next to me was empty. The cold draft from the window hit my face and I was aware that I lost my backpack. I was aghast. Just as I was thinking what to do next, the passenger next to me came back, blood trickling down his chin, and handed me back my bag. He then told me that someone had quietly taken away my bag when I was sleeping. He saw the man and in trying to stop him was hit in his face. The hoodlum escaped, but my bag was retrieved.

I can't explain how deeply ashamed I was of my behaviour – my reticence that bordered on rudeness. The man that I had so obviously mistrusted had made me realise how shallow my behaviour was. I never asked him his name, nor did he ask me mine. But I will never forget him. Ever.

"The world is governed more by appearances than by realities," said American statesman, Daniel Webster. The point is we should not look at a person through the prism of pre-conditioning. It is more important not to make haste and not to judge anyone by his looks.

❐

Be a One-Man Army

In Pune, there used to be a barren hill between the villages of Sus and Baner, its gentle slopes strewn with tufts of grass growing in patches and rocks exposed to open. Today, the hill has undergone a transformation. There are neat ditches created along the hillside and thousands of saplings planted in neat rows that sway and dance with the wind. Various plants like that of banyan, neem, tamarind, sitaphal, amla, Indian fig, guava, mango, jackfruit, jamun and khair are seen in plenty. And this transformation has happened in the last few years. How?

Meet that single man behind this transformation, Bapu Kalmarkar, who works with TELCO Factory in Pune. When Kalmarkar and some other people in his village came to know that the government was considering delimiting the hill, they gathered together to discuss strategies to save the hill. Aggressive reforestation was the strategy planned as forested land was easier to protect than a barren patch. They started digging small hand-made dams. The rainwater stored in those dams helped them to water the saplings easily. These are dams created using the locally available stone to make sure that every last drop of precious rainwater goes back into the earth.

Then an organisation was formed with a few people pooling in their own money. They bought some saplings and planted them. They would work on weekends and after hours to dig holes, build water tanks.

Empty old oil cans and paint buckets are kept besides each tank, so that people from nearby apartments and colonies, who come there for weekends or even for a morning walk, can water the plants. It is like green pilgrimage for many who believe in watering the plants as some believe in feeding the stray dogs. It is a thriving, happy communion of souls, bound together by their love for all things green.

As the barren, craggy hill started transforming before their eyes, more and more people started joining in. The movement was no longer limited to only people from Baner village. People living in the nearby apartments also joined hands. Many of these new entrants were highly educated professionals occupying senior executive level positions. They used their influence to make the greening of the Baner Hill a part of their corporate responsibility initiative.

"A dream doesn't become reality through magic; it takes sweat, determination and hard work," said American statesman, Colin Powell. *Funda* is that if you have that fire in you, then even as a single man, you can save a mountain. And the whole society will follow you.

❒

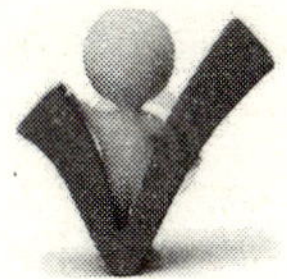

69

Learn to Love

Lawrence Anthony (1950-2012), a legend in South Africa and author of three books, including the bestseller *The Elephant Whisperer*, bravely rescued wildlife and rehabilitated elephants all over the globe from human atrocities, including the courageous rescue of Baghdad Zoo animals during US invasion in 2003. On March 7, 2012, Lawrence Anthony died, leaving behind his wife, two sons and two grandsons and numerous elephants.

Two days after his passing, the wild elephants showed up at his home led by two large matriarchs. Separate wild herds arrived in droves to say goodbye to their beloved man-friend. A total of 20 elephants had patiently walked over 12 miles to get to his South African house. Humans were obviously in awe. Lawrence's wife, Francoise, was especially touched, knowing that the elephants had not been to his house prior to that day for well over a year. Yet, they knew where they were going. The elephants obviously wanted to pay their deep respects, honouring their friend who'd saved their lives - so much respect that they stayed for two days and two nights. Then one morning, they left, making their long journey back home.

Another incident I remember was about a temple elephant in Kerala. He was normally a very docile elephant, but one day, in a fit of rage, he lifted his mahout and threw him to the ground, killing him in the process. The shock of seeing his dead master was very disturbing and he came to his senses almost immediately. So ridden by guilt and sorrow was the elephant, that he stood by his master's side, not letting anybody anywhere near the body, constantly shedding copious tears. He refused food and water for days after this, starving himself till veterinarians tried to force feed him with great difficulty. The elephant began to lose weight. Soon, he died.

That domesticated elephants show great sensitivity and love for humans who give them care is well-known. Unfortunately, humans fail to get the import from such examples and never share such love for their fellow beings.

"Darkness cannot drive out darkness, only light can do that. Hate cannot drive out hate, only love can do that," said American activist, Matin Luther King Jr. True love or affection for anyone can't be hidden. Love and be loved.

❑

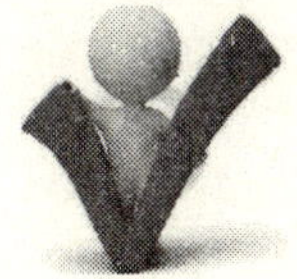

70

Stop to Conquer

Two candidates got selected for a job at a grocery store. On the first day of work, the manager handed them a broom and said, "I want you to sweep the floor."

Now look at the answers the candidates gave:

Candidate 1: "Sir, I am sorry, if the job involves sweeping everyday, let me not disappoint you. I am born with three servants in my house. I did my MBA in retail management and came here to understand the manager's work or managing the retail store. I am certainly not here to sweep the floor. I think the chemistry between me and the organisation may not work. So let me say goodbye to you." And he left.

Candidate 2: After having heard out the first candidate, he was perplexed. First, he thought of leaving the place like the first employee, who was also his good friend. Two SMSes had come from his friend even before he could take a decision. The SMSes read: "Do you still want to work in this shitty place?"

But candidate number 2 quietly took the broom and started sweeping the floor. In his mind, he thought: "Let me see what these guys do with me. I have done the same act when my seniors in college ragged me, so what is new?" The second candidate did everything the manager told him to do that day.

Post lunch he was called and by the same boss and was told that he need not touch the broom from the next day and it was just a test that in case of an emergency arising from a customer dropping something, was he capable enough to clear that area without waiting for the housekeeping department to arrive from a distance? The man became the store manager in six months because he did everything and learnt how they were done. This made him the perfect man to handle the store by himself. Today, he gives the broom to new candidates and asks them to sweep the floor on their first day of duty.

Frankly, if all gifts in life are on shelves – one above the other – then the greatest gifts are on the lowest shelves, one beneath the other. So, it is by stooping lower, we can get the best gifts of life. "Simplicity is the ultimate sophistication," said famous Italian painter, Leonardo da Vinci. We are never happy until we learn the values of simplicity and service.

❐

Choose Values, not Valued Possessions

A story from 1986-87: Years ago, there was a deputy municipal commissioner of the Brihanmumbai Municipal Corporation (BMC), G.R. Khairnar. The post was held by many of his predecessors for almost 50 years or so and none of them achieved any remarkable feat. So what did Khairnar do?

He just did his job. He set about destroying illegal constructions that has sprouted all across the dream city of Mumbai that should have been razed long ago. The slums survived because they enjoyed political patronage in connivance with the slum lords. That was till Khairnar came along and decided to do what he was paid to do. Soon, Khairnar became a hero and remained so till his retirement. Khairnar delivered a message: "Enforcement of law is possible if one had the will to enforce it."

A story from 2012: A 42-year-old Chinese woman, married to a millionaire, gives classes in Chengdu of South-west Sichuan province on "how to attract rich men". She charges $1570 and promises to arrange meetings with rich men as part of the course.

She teaches how to approach rich men, how to date them, when to begin an intimate relationship and when and how to receive a gift. The course also teaches how not to order expensive foods in restaurants, and how rich men favour teachers, doctors and civil servants who are "clean" in their personal habits.

Twenty-five years ago, the society used to appreciate what you did, how you performed in your place of work. People made you a 'Messiah' if you fought for right against the wrong. You were respected because you are an upright officer like G.K. Khairnar. Unfortunately though, years later today, our society values materialistic possessions more than anything else. Little wonder then, youngsters are chasing valued possessions, not values.

"Your habits become your values, your values become your destiny," said Mahatma Gandhi. The fact of the matter is that we should instil values rather than the sense of valued possessions in youngsters. It is futile to blamc our children for chasing material pleasure. They are doing so because we taught them.

❐

72

Be Curious to Learn

During a visit to Switzerland, I went to buy some bread loaf for myself. Upon being informed that there is no brown bread, I asked for white bread. The shopkeeper gave me an astonished look, as if I was illiterate and gave me a verbal download on why white bread should be avoided. That day, I realised that there is so much to learn from a piece of bread that we all take so casually.

The shopkeeper said the Swiss Government has been making people aware of the dangers of eating white bread for decades and in order to get its populace to stop eating it, Switzerland had placed a tax on the purchase of white bread. The tax money is given to bakers to reduce the price of whole wheat bread to encourage people to switch over. The Canadian Government has already passed a law prohibiting the "enrichment" of white bread with synthetic vitamins. Bread must contain the original vitamins found in the grain, not imitations. He also told me that the flour used to make white bread is chemically bleached, just like you bleach your clothes. When you eat white bread, you are also eating the residual chemical bleach. One bleaching agent, chloride oxide, combined with whatever proteins are still left in the flour, produces alloxon. Alloxon is a poison and has been used to produce diabetes in laboratory animals. Chlorine oxide destroys the vital wheat germ oil. It also shortens the shelf life of flour.

Pointing to a board which read: "You can't find good nutrition in white bread, because it is dead bread", the shopkeeper told me about the loss of nutrients in white bread. About 50% of calcium, 70% of phosphorus, 80% of iron, 98% of magnesium, 75% of manganese, 50% of potassium, and 65% of copper is destroyed. If that is not bad enough, about 80% of thiamin, 60% of riboflavin, 75% of niacin, 50% of pantothenic acid, and about 50% of pyridoxine is also lost. On that day, my knowledge of white and brown bread went up by several notches.

What I learned on that day is if you have the inquisitiveness to learn something new, you can learn even from a piece of bread or even while doing some daily chores. "Every man ought to be inquisitive through every hour of his great adventure down to the day when he shall no longer cast a shadow in the sun," said American writer, Frank Moore Colby. The most insignificant of things can teach you a lesson. So, always be ready to learn.

❐

Religious Books Cleanse

An old farmer, who lived in the mountains with his young grandson, used to read the *Bhagavad Gita* every morning. His grandson wanted to be just like him and tried to imitate him in every way he could.

One day the grandson asked, "Grandpa! I try to read the *Bhagavad Gita* just like you but I don't understand it, and what I do understand, I forget as soon as I close the book. What good does reading the *Bhagavad Gita* do?" The farmer, who was putting coal in the stove, quietly turned and said, "Take this coal basket down to the river and bring me back a basket of water."

The boy did as he was told, but all the water leaked before he got back to the house. The grandfather laughed and said, "You'll have to move a little faster next time," and sent him back to the river with the basket to try again.

This time the boy ran faster, but again the basket was empty before he returned home. Out of breath, he told his grandfather that it was impossible to carry water in a basket, and he went to get a bucket instead. The old man said, "I don't want a bucket of water. I want a basket of water. You're just not trying hard enough," and he went out to watch the boy try again.

At this point, the boy knew it was impossible, but he wanted to show his grandfather that even if he ran as fast as he could, the water would leak before he got back to the house. The boy again dipped the basket into the river and ran hard, but when he reached his grandfather, the basket was empty again. Out of breath, he said, "See Grandpa, it's useless!" "So you think it is useless?" The old man said, "Look at the basket." The boy looked at the basket and, for the first time, realised that the basket was different. It had been transformed from a dirty old coal basket and was now clean, inside and outside as it was repeatedly dipped into the water.

"Son, that's what happens when you read the *Bhagavad Gita*. You might not understand or remember everything, but when you read it, you will be cleansed, inside and outside. That is the work of any religious book in our life."

"The transmigration of life takes place in one's own mind. Let one, therefore, keep the mind pure, for what a man thinks that he becomes: this is a mystery of Eternity," says the *Bhagavad Gita*. It's this transmigration of life that reading of religious books tells you about. In doing so, they gradually unravel the mysteries of life, one at a time.

❐

74

The Other India

I remember being part of an impromptu get-together on the arrival of some foreign students to India for an exchange programme. I just asked the students what they felt about India. This is what most of them had to say: "After watching your television programmes, we feel that India is a nation full of traitors, thieves, murderers, terrorists, serial molesters, moral police, corrupt politicians and a cynical citizenry that whips up an occasional righteously indignant reaction."

The big question that came to my mind was: "Is this the India we wish the world to see and inherit?"

I sat down with the students and started telling them good stories happening around the country.

I told them that India is made up of ordinary people doing extraordinary things, like the one Pune technician, who plants trees in his spare time to save a hill, like the frail old lady of 70, who has opened her house and her heart to stray dogs. I told them that India is made of people like the man who after losing his only son of 19 to cancer, used the insurance money to build a home for children, who did not have a home for themselves. It is made of exemplary citizens like the 75-year-old retired scientist, who cycles everywhere because he hates the idea of one more car on the roads of a city that is already bursting at the seams due to air pollution.

India, I told them, belongs to the lady, who teaches music to the maid's kids without charging a single penny. And there are young professional couples, who finance the education of the kids of their society watchmen. People like my household help and her watchman husband form an integral part of India. They have put three boys through college by saving every *paisa* they could from their meager income. "This is OUR India, the India that exists all around us. It is a place where people know how to laugh, where they manage to squeeze some joy out of life's most ordinary moments, no matter how bleak their lives seem to others," I added with a big smile in my face.

Sometimes, just sometimes, let us celebrate this other India, where GOOD does indeed triumph over evil, where life is not an endless litany of whines and complaints. "If I were asked under what sky the human mind has most fully developed some of its choicest gifts, has most deeply pondered on the greatest problems of life, and has found solutions, I should point to India," said German scholar, Max Mueller. Let us take our kids to see this India, so that when they grow up, they know that there is hope. And joy, too.

❐

Motivate Kids for Physical Development

Have you ever applied MIS (Management Information System) on your child's timings? How he/she lives or spends his/her weekly timings? You will get an interesting insight into their functioning. For example, they have 168 hours in a week (I am sure many might have not thought about the figure!). If you give them a basic eight-hour sleep, which is mandatory, that takes away 56 hours and leaves only 112 hours in a week. School takes away Six hours daily and for six days, it consumes 36 hours. The balance is 76 hours. Travelling to school, although it depends on the distance, takes away at least eight hours. The balance is 68 hours.

Home-work takes away 15 hours a week, with roughly 2.30 hours per day. That leaves with just 51 hours in hand. Regular chores like brushing, bathing, eating, doing some *nakhras*, just looking outside the window takes away 21 hours for seven days (three hours a day), which leaves 30 hours in hand for the week.

Now, the villain enters the scene. How much time does your child spend in watching the television? In a working couple's house, the child watches anything between 20 to 26 hours in a week. This includes playing on your mobile phones and also playing video games on the TV or otherwise. This leaves just four hours for play. So, tell me, when do you think the children can really go for physical development? Look at the figures from the other side. When the children of this generation reach the second standard, a survey says their weight is at least 30% more than the children of their age 20 years ago. With just four hours of play in a week, what can you expect?

I remember, as a child, my family made a conscious decision not to buy a television set. When cable TV invaded the country, my grandfather, a retired army officer, was adamant on not buying an idiot box as his constant refrain was: "how much can you monitor kids?"

Frankly, I am not trying to make a case for making life TV-free. I understand it is an important source of information and entertainment. All I am trying to stress is that one must try to develop a sense of judgement in the kids where they can differentiate between a couch potato and a physically well-developed young person. "Change yourself and fortune will change with you," says a Portuguese proverb. Think about it.

❐

76

If One Door Closes, Others Open

In 1995, Mohammedi Abdulla Dalal was happy when his wife delivered a baby girl. That pride made him to name her Zainab, which means daughter of a proud father. Little Zainab Dalal's parents were not aware that their little one can never hear them calling her by her name. She never responded to any sound. Thus, she never picked up a single word. That affected her speech too. The three-year-old girls always used to sit with a piece of paper and quietly draw what she saw. Though it improved her drawing, the concern revolved around speech and hearing. That shook the parents, but they did not lose their heart. Apart from medical attention, they sent her to the Central Society for the Education of Deaf in Mumbai.

Zainab, however, wanted to make her father proud. She told her parents that she wanted to go to a 'regular' school. She worked hard from the standard one to get a certificate from her current school, which certifies that "she is eligible for 'regular' school". But the road was tough. Every principal shut his door firmly on her face and she almost lost hope. It was then that the local media stepped into the scene in 2004. Following their crusade, Zainab got admission to a prestigious school called Young Ladies High School Fountain in Mumbai.

Then began another battle. The school teachers knew that if they had to go to a section where Zainab was studying, they needed to put in extra effort of writing everything on the board because she couldn't hear. Other students felt that the class was really slow because everything was being written down. The teachers had a tough time, but two of Zainab's friends, Mehwish and Nagma helped her out after the class. In 2012, Zainab made everyone proud by scoring distinction marks of 75.67% in SSC. The road was paved for her to scale greater heights.

Remember: If God closes one door on you, He opens many others to scrape through to success. "A pessimist sees the difficulty in every opportunity; an optimist sees the opportunity in every difficulty," said former UK Prime Minister, Winston Churchill. It is up to us how we use the opportunities to our advantage.

❐

Fight for a Just Cause

Saurabh Kumar alias Chabila Paswan is a poor Dalit from Halaiya village situated in Vaishali district near Patna in Bihar. He was also landless and under some government norms, was trying hard to get some land for himself and the family. The moment the local goons sensed this, they posed as a huge threat to him and his family. Paswan claimed that they tried to eliminate him. This threat made him to seek police help and he went to the police station to lodge a complaint against the high and mighty.

The ordeal began with the cops asking him to sit outside the police station for hours. Then he was told that the inspector of the station has gone away for some urgent government duty and asked him to visit the next day. The ritual of giving some excuses continued for some days, and when they saw Paswan was relentless and refused to move out of the station, the police-in-charge called him inside to hear his side of the story. After hearing him out, the in-charge of the police post allegedly asked him for a bribe of ₹ 1,000. But when he said that the money is not required to lodge a complaint, the in-charge apparently told him to seek some legal help if he is so much confident about the government rules.

Paswan went home, made some placards which explained why he is begging and went around the streets asking for alms. His wife and children went along with him. His innovative way of handling the high and mighty attracted the attention of the locals, who joined him in a big way to beg for alms for bribing government officials. After collecting ₹ 1,000, Paswan went to the post office, bought 10 postal orders worth ₹ 100 and sent them to the Chief Minister by speed-post in a closed envelope along with a detailed petition on what made him to do this. He requested Chief Minister, Nitish Kumar, to pay the amount to the corrupt police officer, who had asked for it. By sheer grit, Paswan stood up to a just cause and emerged victorious. "If my mind can conceive it, and my heart can believe it, I know I can achieve it," said an American civil rights activist, Jesse Jackson. The message in the story is instead of cursing the system and fate, work your way out. It will not only take you to the top, but, in some cases, make you a hero.

❐

Keep the Fire of Will Burning

Kanaram Meena, belonging to an SC community, was a watchman in the IAS Colony in Gandhi Nagar situated on Tonk Road of the Jaipur city. He worked for almost 20 years in that position at different IAS/IPS bungalows. Being a watchman, he was getting his duty orders everyday to guard some IAS officers. He was always impressed the way these officers conducted themselves, spoke to their subordinates and treated their children. The old man always dreamt that his son, Prahlad Narayan Meena should either become an IAS or an IPS officer. Unfortunately though, fate had some other plan. He died in 1995, when Parhlad was in the seventh standard.

The sudden death of his father not only forced Prahlad to mature before his age but also made him move back to his village, Rampura, which is 40 kms from Jaipur. His mother always kept her husband's dream afire by constantly reminding Prahlad about his aim. But the lack of financial support forced Prahlad to go for work, which affected his studies.

Then came his brother-in-law, who worked in the Secretariat in Jaipur and who opted to take Prahlad back with him for further studies. He was admitted in a private school. Prahlad gradually gained focus, his grades improved and he topped the 12th standard. Prahlad did his BA, followed by a BEd degree. In 2008, he got the job of a trained Graduate teacher in English with the Delhi government. This improved his economic situation. He sent his mother to various religious trips that she always desired.

But his woes did not end. Land grabbers went after his piece of land in the village. Prahlad was livid. He knew becoming a police officer was the only way to fight the goons in his village. He longed to compete in the civil services. He started preparing himself for the civil services examinations. In August 2011, he pre-qualified and in May 2012, cleared his final examinations. He proceeded to Moussorie in August 2012 for his police training.

"The will is the keystone in the arch of human achievement," said the American author, Thomas Parker Boyd. The point is if you keep your aim afire in your belly, you can easily realise your dream. The hunger to achieve your dream must always be there till one reach the destination.

❐

79

The New Education Mantra

Several schools in London follow a technique that will put many of us in an ambivalent position. You may love it for its ability to provide freedom and, at the same time, you may hate it for its ability to confuse you. They just flip the classroom to the homework environment and vice-versa. This means that they ask the students to do homework in the class and classwork at home. The methodology is called "flipped classroom format".

In India, R.N. Poddar School, situated at Santa Cruz in Mumbai, switched over to "flipped classroom format" (FCF) in 2012. In this format, all homework for the students will be done in the school, while all classroom syllabuses will be learnt at home. As part of this system, a flipped classroom inverts traditional teaching methods by delivering instructions online outside the class and moving the homework into the class.

In a traditional classroom, the teacher teaches and it is mostly one-way communication for larger part of the period. Because of the constant monitoring, the students are not permitted even to form their opinion, because the teacher may restrict that with his/her body language. So, the school decided to record all subjects' lectures earlier and provide that through a link to the student, who can log on and listen to that lecture on his/her computer. The student can note down all his/her doubts and discuss the same in the classroom with the teacher. This methodology allows the student to discuss more in class, which was earlier a monologue from the teacher's side.

For six months, the school practised this in class VII and, based on the learning, they adopted this new technology with slight modifications. Thus, lectures can take place now either through videos, Internet or video conferencing. The teachers also sometimes pop-up in the social networking sites to see what doubts the subjects are rising among their students. This makes the students comfortable and because the teachers are on the social networking sites, the chemistry between them also improves.

The common feeling among the students about homework is "forced on us and we are not able to go out to play". With the FCF, homework will be fun and the monologue, which is a lecture, remains there where it was earlier.

"Education is not the filling of a pail, but the lighting of a fire," said the Irish poet, William Butler Yeats. If you really want the essence of education to penetrate cent percent into each young brain that comes to school, you should keep experimenting with new methods and processes that would enhance the learning ability of the younger generation.

❐

80

Listen to the Less Qualified Employee

This real story took place over 30 years ago. Pradeep Shinde, woıking as a machine operator in a leading tractor-producing company (name of the operator and the company changed and withheld to protect their identity) had only done his HSC, which was the then 11th standard school final.

Shinde was young and just had joined the factory. The factory is still located at the Kandivili suburb in Mumbai just along the railway station, as a separate railway track is laid to take away the tractors from the manufacturing plant to the interiors of the country, where they are needed for agricultural purpose.

A Cincinnati Milacron Machine was imported from Germany for their tractor plant. After an initial opening ceremony, etc., the machine was put into operation. The Germans came to the factory, installed it all through the night for almost one month and left after a day of testing. Here, it is pertinent to say that the day of testing was Sunday and the railways had stopped the suburban trains for 12 hours for maintenance work, which is normal in Mumbai.

A few days after operation, the machine developed a snag. The engineers did their best, but to no avail. Pradeep, who was working on the machine, used to sleep sometime next to the machine after a long day work of 18 hours. He once woke up to the siren of a long distance night train passing through the station and observed there was a huge vibration on the floor. It struck him that the vibration might have made the machine faulty. The operator gave a suggestion to the engineers to rebuild the foundation.

No one listened to him. The senior German engineer team, which was later specially flown in, found some point in his statement. They checked the foundation by monitoring it for all 24 hours and for three consecutive days. The German team came up with the solution of dismantling the existing foundation by shifting the machine. They built a new foundation and installed the machine at a distance slightly away from the current location, where one cannot hear the vibrations when trains are speeding by. Following the change, the machine never gave any problem.

Shinde was later rewarded as he had proved even an ordinary man in a company can lend innovative insights into the job.

"Everyone, who's ever taken a shower, has had an idea. It's the person who gets out of the shower, dries off and does something about it, who makes a difference," said the American entrepreneur, Nolan Bushnell. Strategic thinking can take place at all levels. It is wrong to think that strategy is limited to the higher echelons. Many organisational changes have been born out of strategic inputs from the area or branch levels.

❐

81

Keep the Moral Fabric Stain-Free

Prabhaker T. Vaidya was invited to the National Freedom Fighter's Convention held in Panaji many years ago, which was inaugurated by the then Prime Minister, Chandrashekhar. After the speeches, it was time to table motions. There were many that were announced, largely symbolic motions expressing the official freedom fighter's line on issues that were facing the country. Finally, the most important motion of the day was put to vote, the motion that asked for an increase in the facilities extended to the freedom fighters and the amount of pension the state conferred on them.

It was a motion that was expected to be carried unanimously. After all, did the freedom fighters not deserve all the respect and facilities that they got? There were a thousand heads nodding in agreement as the motion was being tabled. The motion was about to be passed with voice voting, when the person, who was chairing the session, asked if anyone in the audience was against the motion. It was more of a formality, as no one expected any person in the audience to voice a contrary opinion.

There was, however, one dissenting voice among the 3,000 odd people gathered at the convention. That voice belonged to Prabhker T. Vaidya. "I oppose the motion", he said. After the initial few moments of shock, one could feel an angry murmur building through the crowd like a wave. The chairperson asked Prabhakerji if he wanted to state his objection on stage so everyone could hear it. "Freedom fighters should not act like beggars. We are warriors," he started. His very first sentence created a furore. The entire convention was on its feet now, heckling, booing, shouting Prabhakerji down. He tried to continue, but his voice was drowned by the angry shouts of the crowd. Someone from the stage grabbed the microphone from him and he was forced to come down.

Prabhakerji was actively involved in the Goan freedom struggle. He played a key role in the liberation of Dadra and Nagar Haveli and led several attacks on police stations and armouries in Goa, including successful attacks on the Cuncolim and Canacona police outposts. He struck such terror in the hearts of the Portuguese authorities that the Portuguese Government tried him twice *in absentia*. He was sentenced to over 35 years of rigorous imprisonment, but he was the elusive hero.

In 1961, when Goa was freed, Prabhakerji could have had the pick of positions of power in the newly formed Union Territory of Goa, Daman and Diu. Many of his erstwhile colleagues joined the police force or other state departments, while some participated in active electoral politics. Prabhakerji, however, turned down all offers to return to his native village of Cuncolim, this time to liberate his people from the shackles of ignorance. Joining hands with other like-minded people, he started the Cuncolim Educational Society.

Cuncolim United High School was born with a handful of students and a small band of dedicated teachers. Vaidya couple were one of the first teachers at the school. While male Vaidya accepted a modest honorarium, his life partne taught English without taking a single rupee as remuneration. Despite having dedicated the best decade of his life to the Goan freedom struggle, Prabhakerji never capitalised on it. He never applied for the government pension granted to the freedom fighters nor did he avail of any other facilities like discounted travel. He never even bothered to collect the *Tamrapatra* conferred upon him by the Central Government.

In his 77 years, he always heard to the voice of his own conscience and none else.

"Always do what is right. It will gratify half of mankind and astound the other," said the American author, Mark Twain. Heed this: Even if you cannot keep the moral fabric as spotless as Prabhakerji, the least you can do is to keep it free of major stains using his stories as a cleanser.

(This story was shared by Prabhaker T. Vaidya's daughter, Shefali Vaidya.)

❐

82

Brain vs. Conscience Who do You Listen To?

In Mahabharata, Duryodhana was a formidable opponent for Bhima, aiming his own blows with skill and evading his adversary with dexterity. It seemed as if the victory that the Pandavas had been so sure of winning was slipping from their hands, for even Bhima was no match for the desperate Duryodhana.

When the duo fought, Krishna made a sign to Bhima, touching his own thigh, and suddenly Bhima remembered the vow he had made that he would break Duryodhana's thighs. He remembered in a flash the game of dice, and the shaming of Draupadi. Red hot anger filled Bhima, and disregarding the rule of war that the enemy may not strike below the navel, Bhima lifted his mighty mace and struck at Duryodhana's thighs and broke them. With a cry of reproach and pain, Duryodhana fell to the ground, bleeding. Then Bhima, in a savage, mad frenzy, put his foot upon the fallen man's head and danced triumphantly, so that all around stood horror struck. Yudhishthira rebuked him, saying, "Do not trample upon him, Bhima, for Duryodhana is your cousin and a prince. Whatever his faults, whatever our suffering, your conduct is not worthy of a Kshatriya!"

But Duryodhana, lying upon the ground waiting for his death, laughed at Yudhishthira's words. "Let him trample upon my head, Yudhishthira. This is not the only unworthy, low act he, you and the other Pandavas have committed. Why, you have won the war, but you cannot deny that you have done so only through unfair means and unrighteous conduct. Bhishma, Drona and Karna were slain through foul dishonesty. Jayadratha was destroyed by trickery, deceit and cunning. And do you think I did not see Krishna making a sign to Bhima, urging him to hit me upon my thighs? When have you acted in accordance with the Kshatriya code, that you rebuke Bhima now?"

Fierce were the emotions that the dying Duryodhana voiced, and to the end, he remained implacable and unbending. Yet, though much of what he said was true, he forgot his own part in the great tragedy. He did not see that his jealousy and hatred, as much as the Pandavas' wrongdoings, had been at the root of the evil that had befallen everyone - the death of brave warriors, the crumbling of a mighty empire.

When I used to read the Mahabharata as a young lad, on many occasions, I felt that many characters were deeply wronged against. I always felt that Lord Krishna has been the prime instigator behind many such acts, one may call unethical and deceitful practices, which gave the Pandavas an edge and advantage over the Kauravas. I used to be astounded that a God in human persona would do such un-God-like things. I felt that his whole human *avatar* has several episodes that use unethical means to achieve ethical goals.

"Educating the mind without educating the heart is no education at all," said the Greek philosopher, Aristotle. The emphasis is on the conflict between conscience and brain. One's conscience would say 'no'. But the brain would analyse the situation, evaluate the seriousness of the possible good, whether a larger number of people are going to benefit by that decision to use unethical means, and say 'yes'.

❐

83

Always say 'Thanks' It's Our Culture

For just getting a paper from the main hall to my bedroom, I have thanked my daughter every time she does that mundane work. And if sometimes while attending a phone call, if I had forgotten to give those customary thanks to her, she would stand like a statue and would say "you have forgotten to say something". I will immediately apologize and, with a smile, say 'thanks'. She will hop on to her tricycle and would go back to her play.

This used to happen more than 20 years ago, but even today she expects me to graciously appreciate the small errand job she does with a single word called "thanks" or two words "thank you". She never got tired of that word nor I of repeating it.

In Sevagram Gandhiji's ashram near Wardha in Maharashtra, where I spent a large part of my childhood, on Independence Day, the elders in the ashram were thanked by the children for getting them the independence they are enjoying. There were many seniors and elders, who were part of the independence moment and went to jail for months and years for protesting against the British Raj. I always bowed when I would pass by the *Amar Jawan Jyoti* situated near the India Gate in New Delhi for protecting this country. I never had an inkling how I could say 'thanks' to them, until I chanced upon a website 'www.21fools.com' run from Jaipur in Rajasthan, which does the job similar to my thought. The site sends cards to all the soldiers for a fee of ₹ 50. For this purpose, it has tied up with the Indian Army and some leading corporate houses. Although our soldiers know that we are thankful to them for their bravery, it is sometimes essential to say it.

"As we express our gratitude, we must never forget that the highest appreciation is not to utter words, but to live by them," said the former US President, John F. Kennedy. You know, thanking is a good management practice. And thanking need not be in words. It can be by way of action, smile, gesture or a simple gift or card. Other than our 'veer jawans', shouldn't we remember great entrepreneurs like J.R.D. Tata and Dhirubhai Ambani on their birthdays? Shouldn't we remember Milkha Singh for his contribution whenever Olympics is organised? Thanking once in a while all those people responsible for our happy living is part of our culture, isn't it?

❐

SECTION-V

Future's Waiting. Brace for it

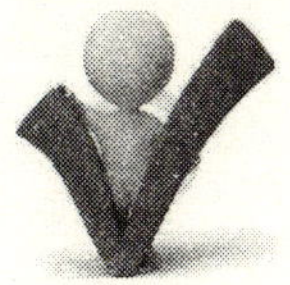

84

You have to Decide When Life Offers Temptations

In 1967, Maj. Gen. Dhruv C. Katoch, now the Additional Director, Centre for Land Warfare Studies (CLAWS), was then a 16-year-old child. His father was a colonel in the Army. Except for the huge government bungalow in Ajmer, the family had no car, no scooter and no refrigerator. However, the family felt no sense of deprivation and the lack of amenities. The family always took a rickshaw and never took the official car for personal work.

One evening, however, junior Katoch mustered the courage and asked his father, "Why don't you let us use the office jeep sometimes, Dad?" The colonel turned, looked at his son straight in his eyes and said, "I would son, but the pear would not go down my throat." "What pear?" the son asked.

The colonel waited a while and then narrated this most amazing tale. "When I was a kid of your age," he said, "I had gone out to play with my friends. There was a beautiful orchard where the first lot of pears had ripened on the trees, which we could not resist. We crawled under the fence, took all we could carry before scampering back to safety. I took my share of the loot home." The colonel continued: "Your grandfather was sitting on his favourite chair on the verandah smoking his *hookah*. I offered him a plate with the freshly cut fruit. Your grandfather must have guessed the source of the offering and its method of procurement, but he didn't say anything about that to me. He simply said, "My son, this pear would not go down my throat," as he found it impossible to eat anything that had not been honestly obtained. "There was no admonishment in his tone, no anger, just a quiet statement of fact."

The young lad took the plate back with an overriding sense of pain and guilt. Away from his father's eyes, took a bite of the pear to see if there was any truth in the assumption. Well, the pear didn't go down his throat either. So, next morning, the colonel confessed to the orchard owner. The owner kept his arm on his shoulder and presented him a basket of fresh ripe pears. There was silence for some time, then the colonel continued and told junior Katoch, "Life offers many temptations, son, but some of us cannot get the pear down our throats."

"If you do not tell the truth about yourself, you cannot tell it about other people," said the English writer, Virginia Woolf. Life does offer many temptations. Which to accept and which not to, is a call you must take.

❒

Only Unmatched Efforts Bring Appreciation

Shankar Baba Papalkar is the father of 125 children. He lives in a place called Wazaar near Amravati in Maharashtra. He has been running an *ashram* for disabled orphans since 1992.

Shankar is their biological father but has given his name to the 125 children, most of whom are mentally-challenged. Moreover, unlike other remand homes, no inmate is asked to leave the centre after he/she turns 18. Baba, as he is fondly called by the orphans, believes that the deaf and dumb, mentally-challenged and children with multiple disability cannot fend for themselves even after attaining the age of 18. He believes that the girl children, who attain 18 and asked to leave the orphanage, generally end up in the prostitution business and the males take to begging. Baba picks up orphan children from dustbins, railway stations, temples and even accepts children rescued by the police.

Over 60% of the children in his *ashram* have zero IQ. This means that he has to carry them from toilet onwards till back to bed in the night. He does that with utmost care, love and responsibility. Of the 40% disabled children, he has managed to get government jobs for 14 of them. Most important is the fact that Baba has managed to get

14 disabled girls married. According to him, science has proved that children born to mentally-challenged mothers are the smartest and they take care of the mothers. Apart from his responsibilities, Baba finds time to meet politicians and requests them to amend the laws for orphanages like the one run by him by inserting a word '*laawaris*, which will ensure permanent shelter for children even after they attain the age of 18.

Many of us, who have been blessed with proper body and mind, have been doing many charities and taking care of many needs of the poor and the needy. But we may have been doing it in spare time; not like Baba who has devoted his whole life to the cause.

"If you can't excel with talent, triumph with effort," said radio talk show host, Dave Weinbaum. The human race, which always looks for appreciation, should understand that to get recognised in any job or any field of work, one needs to put in relentless and unmatched efforts.

❐

86 Keep the Fire of Curiosity Burning

Pritish Patil, the wizard to crack the international Olympiad, earned laurels once again for the nation after he bagged a silver medal at the Biology International Olympiad held in Taipei in 2011. Earlier, Pritish Patil, as a student of 12th science in Nashik in Maharashtra, won the silver medal at the international Olympiad in Astronomy. Pritish's success story does not end here. He was selected to represent India at his third international Olympiad in 2011, this time his subject being Earth Science. Pritish is the only student to have been so consistently selected in different subjects as part of the Indian team.

What makes Pritish's achievement special is that he studied all on his own, without any classes or guidance. He used the Internet and Internet forums to become smart. His journey to the study of astronomy began when, as a student of class 6, he was gifted an encyclopedia by his uncle. He was so intrigued by the information on planets and black holes that it made him read further and his curiosity in the subject took him to the study of it. This process took a major leap when he was introduced to the vast knowledge on astronomy through the Internet.

Since childhood, Pritish had been a bright student. The confidence in his abilities grew after he started getting success in various competitive exams. But Pritish's family thought differently. His parents wanted him to enjoy what he learnt and that he should find interest in knowledge. They never pressured him for marks or ranks.

When kids of his age focussed merely on the syllabus, Pritish was busy satisfying his curiosity. He researched and learnt different subjects like physics and mathematics that were necessary for astronomy. Studying on his own, Pritish needed a lot of self-discipline, consistency and focus. "That came by naturally and I didn't do anything special for it, as I felt an inner desire for studying and knowing. The desire kept me going," Pritish said in an interview.

"The important thing is not to stop questioning. Curiosity has its own reason for existing," said the German physicist, Albert Einstein. What's driven home by Pritish's example is that it's essential to look beyond course books and school syllabi. One must have the constant itch of curiosity to excel in life.

❑

87

Look at a Problem from All Angles

Dinesh Khandelwal owns Khandelwal Motors Private Limited in a place called Mahua in Dosa district situated exactly in the centre of Jaipur-Agra Road. In a conversation with me, he shared a story which has huge ramifications on management practice.

His mother had some major ailment in her uterus and needed surgical intervention. She was rushed and operated upon and was advised medicine for at least next six months. Dinesh obviously picked up the medicines for the first fortnight thinking that he would keep buying them locally as and when the situation warrants. Upon reaching his hometown, Dinesh was back to business. Suddenly, he remembered the next course of medicine for his mother. His efforts failed as the nearby chemists did not have the stock.

The first thing he did was that he made six photocopies of the prescription and gave it to five friends who travelled to nearby metros on business tours. The first friend did not come back for the next three days and when asked, said it had completely slipped out of his mind. The second friend apparently bought the medicines, but failed to deliver them. The third and the fourth did not turn up. It was the fifth friend who not only bought the medicines and delivered them, but also advised him that a particular medicine was not supposed to be taken with milk. Dinesh immediately called up the surgeon who wrote the prescription and he too confirmed the same and apologized that he had forgotten to write the same.

Dinesh recalled that this fifth friend of his—Ramesh—was apparently doing very well in his business. That is purely because he had the foresight of covering one job—however simple it may seem—from all 360 degrees. That left no possibility unattended.

"Management is efficiency in climbing the ladder of success; leadership determines whether the ladder is leaning against the right wall," said the American author, Stephen Covey. Remember, whatever job you do, if you secure it from all sides and do not leave behind any unfinished section of the same work, you are bound to win the heart of your boss.

❐

Give a Corporate Look to Education Business

If I say at least 16,500 hours of teaching time are wasted in each college with 100 teachers each year, one may think that the teachers are either not teaching or that the students are bunking the classes. But that's not the case. I realised this on one of my visits to a college called Graduate School of Business (GSB) in Indore. Actually, one can increase the teaching time by just reworking his teaching methodology.

Every teacher spends the first 10 minutes in explaining what she or he is going to teach in the class which runs for 50 minutes to one hour. This may or may not include manual attendance marking in colleges. Two minutes of spoken explanation and eight minutes of written explanation, which they take to write the relevant subject of the day on the white board. If every teacher takes five lectures a day, then he or she spends 50 minutes in explaining what is going to be taught during a particular period, and in a week of six days, they spend 300 minutes explaining the topics. And for an average of 200 working days in a year, teachers spend 10,000 working minutes which is some 166 hours doing this. If 100 teachers are doing the same thing each day, an educational institution has lost 16,666 hours of teaching time a year.

What Graduate School of Business (GSB) has done is that it has put all course materials of each class and each teacher in an audio-visual equipment and the screen gets operational in each class the moment the teacher enters the class. The teacher only reads out the line which takes less than two minutes and does not waste time in writing the same on the board with a marker, which consumes at least eight minutes. If calculated in the same manner as mentioned above, it adds up to 133 hours of teaching time for each teacher each year, and for 100 teachers, it's a saving of 133,333 hours for the whole year.

Each teacher can carry small biometric attendance equipment, like credit card charging machine. The machine can either be placed in one place or circulated among students to mark their attendance even when the class is on without disturbing anyone.

These small changes in an education business can enhance teaching time of the faculty and, thus, will have a huge impact in the long run. More teaching time means more knowledge, more intelligence pumped into the system that eventually makes better students. And only an able teacher can do it. "A teacher affects eternity; he can never tell where his influence stops," said, American journalist, Henry B. Adams.

So, think sharp. If you give a corporate look to education business and view every aspect of it the way corporate houses do, it would eventually lead to growth for both the students and the educational institute promoters.

❐

Sacrifice has No Boundaries

Her world crashed like a pack of cards when she heard the news. A few months before her daughter's marriage came the shocker that the prospective groom's father had a fatal liver failure and his days were numbered if replacement wasn't done instantly.

The groom was shattered, ready to donate his liver to save his father. Which meant that for Sangeeta Sharma (name changed on request), a brilliant reporter with a leading Hindi national daily, who had so meticulously arranged for her daughter's marriage, would live to see her child devastated. That's when the scribe, who is in her mid-40s, unhesitatingly decided to chip in to make a sacrifice which would turn the clock back. The decision was to be taken in 24 hours and she decided to donate the most part of her own liver—70%—to the groom's father. She did, which changed the old man's life. Her own, of course, was never to be the same again.

Sangeeta's decision, which she made with a smile, saved no less than three lives. At an age when one begins to climb the stairs of professional success and yearns for peace, she garnered the courage to make the sacrifice, all at her own cost. The newspaper went ahead to offer her a desk job, as donating 70% of her liver left her movements severely restricted. She neither grudges her "infirmity", nor does she think she has done anything great. "It's just that my daughter and son-in-law have miles to go. I am satisfied," I recall her telling me.

In a world given to flash and flamboyance, where sensitivity and sacrifice find no shelter, Sangeeta's action deserves to be recognised more than anything else. I remember the words of Mahatma Gandhi, who said, "The sacrifice which causes sorrow to the doer of the sacrifice is no sacrifice. Real sacrifice lightens the mind of the doer and gives him/her a sense of peace and joy." Though we live in a time, and in a nation, largely consumed by hatred, it would be a mistake to assume there is no stomach for sacrifice—or its sister virtue, service—in our society. Sangeeta's example corroborates that the heart is still where it should be. And who says service and sacrifice can be rendered only at the nation's borders? Today, we need the virtues to show even among ourselves. People like Sangeeta are God's gift to show the way.

❐

No Alternative to Dedication

Both were at their prime age of 18, both were doing the same course, both were appearing for the same competitive courses, both made their family and their village very proud, both are children of poverty-stricken parents, and yet, both applied for a scholarship to study in the United States. The strongest thread that bound them was their dream—to make it in life and come back to help their respective villages so that they prosper.

They do not know each other because their respective villages are miles apart, although they are from the same state of Maharashtra and share the same mother tongue. The common factor for these two village girls was hard work and dedication to their studies that made them gain a scholarship to a US varsity. Both the girls had to undergo a tough selection process. They were shortlisted from among 50 students belonging to the rural areas of Maharashtra. The selection process, spread over 10 months, was carried out with the help of an NGO. Karishma Randhve of Shirwal village in Satara district and Anjani Lahane from Mangaon village in Raigad district, have been selected by the University of Cincinnati (UC) in Ohio, US, as the maiden recipients of the global opportunity scholarship introduced by the varsity.

India is the first-ever beneficiary country of the UC scholarship initiative. While Karishma is the daughter of a labourer, Anjani's father is a farmer. But poor financial conditions did not stop the parents from educating these girls. The duo received full scholarships, including tuition, housing, meals and air fare for a total value of ₹ 67.50 lakh each to pursue their engineering degrees at UC in 2012. The director of international admissions at UC, Jonathan Weller, was in India to escort the students to the varsity.

Karishma completed her primary education from Dnyansamvardhini High School in Shirwal. She used to give tuitions to pay for her studies. Anjani did her SSC from a school in Mangaon. While Karishma will pursue engineering in the bio-medical stream, computer engineering will be Anjani's subject.

"To become a master at any skill, it takes the total effort of your heart, mind and soul working together in tandem," said stage artiste, Maurice Young. You will agree that there is no alternative to dedication. If you are focussed on one subject called success, then you can surmount the most insurmountable hindrances. If Karishma and Anjani have proved it, so can you.

❐

91

Do Good to Get Back Good

Some time ago, while returning home late in the night, Jagdish Patel, Head, University Project, New Initiative Group, ICFAI, University of Gujarat was stopped by a cop, who asked him for his driving licence. On mentioning that he had forgotten it at home, he was told to meet the police inspector sitting near the check-post. Patel met the police inspector, who said he knew Patel well as one who conducted various career guidance seminars. The inspector said he would condone Patel, but had a request. He asked Patel to conduct similar seminars for children of the police personnel at the police staff housing colony located under his jurisdiction.

On Patel's acceptance, a career guidance seminar was organised at the police welfare centre. It gave Patel an opportunity to interact with some 180 children, whose parents were working in various police departments. Patel later told me he had a wonderful experience with the children. They asked him many pointed questions regarding further studies, career options, future prospects and salary expectations. Patel did his best to answer the queries to their satisfaction relying upon his corporate and academic exposure. In the process, he tried to put the seeds of 'Think Big' in their fertile minds by giving many examples. At the end of the session, he could see the glow of satisfaction in their eyes as if they were now ready to conquer their bright future. Patel told me that it was this glow that was his true remuneration.

The news that Patel had conducted the seminar reached the Chief Minister's Office, which, in turn, sent him a request that he conduct such seminars at the police staff welfare centres all over Gujarat. The direct fallout of the request from the CM's Office was that Patel started getting requests from various cities of Gujarat, asking him for convenient dates to conduct seminars.

"Grace was in all her steps. Heav'n in her eye; in every gesture dignity and love," said the English poet, John Milton. Get the *funda*? A small human gesture comes back to you as rewards, which are many times more than what you have given others.

❐

92

Be Determined Never Give Up

It was sometime in 1970s that Kiran Bedi became the first woman to take charge as an IPS officer. There was a small riot in Sadar Bazaar in New Delhi. The then police commissioner told Bedi to take 20 men and rush to the spot. While moving to Sadar Bazaar, the commissioner on the radio updated her that the miscreants had torched a house in which at least 20 people were trapped. When Bedi and her team reached the spot, she could see people screaming from inside and the fire was too big to douse.

Bedi ordered her constables to break the door. But none dared. She then asked one of her constables to pour water on her and drench her. With the wet uniform, she went near the door, broke and entered the house. Lifting a lady on her shoulders, she brought her out to safety. The moment the constables saw their lady officer daringly entering the torched house, they were enthused. Pouring water on their self, the constables entered the house and rescued all 17 occupants, of whom Bedi had saved seven.

There is another story about Bedi of how she used basic common sense when she was the head of Delhi traffic. Her logic was that if the roads are wide and can take two to three lanes on each side, why should parked vehicles block roads meant for the common public? In one of the busy junctions, when she realised that the common man is not able to move even his/her scooter, she asked for a crane. In those days, Delhi police had just two cranes and both were under repair. She sought private cranes, but the question was who would pay for them. Bedi stood as a guarantee and said if the government does not pay, she would pay for them from her salary.

Private cranes were brought to the scene and, in a few days, the whole of Delhi was terrorised when it saw a crane on the road.

People started following road rules and parked vehicles only in parking zones. In fact, she once refused to let go of a car belonging to the Prime Minister's Office, which was parked on the wrong side. Despite pleas from the commissioner, she refused to budge under political pressure.

Nothing is impossible if you are determined enough. "Courage is the most important of all the virtues, because without courage, you can't practise any other virtue consistently," said the American author, Maya Angelou. The problem is we tend to give up too easily. Stick to your aim, come what may and see yourself wade through troubles.

❐

93

Never say Retire

Born in 1916, she is currently the consulting president of a bank. Yet she travels to all her meetings and seminars in the municipal bus service of Pune which is called PMT. The driver allows her to board from the front and somebody eventually would offer her a seat no sooner than she gets into the bus.

That's because people know that Rukhmani Shitole at this age is still travelling for business and not for pleasure. She has never missed a single meeting of Jijamata Mahila Bank and Santulan Trust so far. A native of Kolewadi village in Theur Taluka of Pune district, Rukhmani who is a great-grandmother, is the oldest living person of her village.

It is interesting to note that in her school days, Rukhmani not only ranked first throughout, but also studied till standard seven, unheard of then. Married at the age of 12 to Kondiba who was very *avant-gard*e and active in politics, Rukhmani Shitole learnt about public life and services from her husband. Kondiba and Rukhmani had one daughter from their marriage. Kondiba married for the second time to have a son. From that marriage, he had three sons and two daughters. Their children and grandchildren are looking after Rukhmani now.

When the family settled down, Rukhmani decided to be part of public life. She contested the gram panchayat elections in 1962 and won by two votes. Her education helped her to understand the plight of women and she started a Mahila Sanstha and Ganesh Doodh Utpadak Sanstha for the empowerment of women and to help them survive on milk business. She then contested the zilla parishad elections in 1972 and won. She was a panchayat samiti member for 12 years and, now, she is the consulting president of Jijamata Bank.

When she is not attending meetings, she would be busy opening the wedding cards or greeting cards from various people who consider her the first citizen of the village. Many come and take her blessings before digging a well or starting a new business or leaving for higher education to Pune. And when she is done with her meetings and meeting visitors, she spends her spare time in the beautiful kitchen garden she has developed. All vegetables for her family are grown there and nobody goes to the bazaar to buy any.

Remember what French author, Antoine de Saint-Exupery said, "True happiness comes from the joy of deeds well done, the zest of creating things anew." Rukhmani has proved that no one can retire you from leading an active life, age notwithstanding. All you need is the passion for work and the zest for life.

❐

94

Perception can Cut Both Ways

It was a day after *Raksha Bandhan* festival in Mumbai. The special court, headed by the Judge M.L. Tahaliyani, who was appointed specially to handle the 26/11 carnage, opened to hear the witnesses involved in the gory saga that shook the nation and the world at large. As Ajmal Kasab stood quietly in a corner, his lawyer told the court that his client was curious to know why men were wearing a thread on their wrists.

Judge Tahaliyani, who has the reputation of being very vocal, asked the lawyer what he told his client. The lawyer said he told him that this was a sacred thread that sisters tied to the wrists of their brothers as a mark of love. To this, Kasab reportedly asked him if his sister could tie a thread to his wrist. The lawyer apparently told Kasab that in this country, not merely one's own sister, but any woman could tie a *rakhi* to the wrist of a person she regarded as her brother.

The media splashed this news item the next day, giving the perception that Kasab was, after all, a nice human being at heart. I remember how the news diluted the anger of the people against a person who did not show mercy even to kids.

The sympathy wave continued until advocate Ujjwal Nikam, the special public prosecutor for the Government of Maharashtra, who is known for fighting cases of celebrities like actor Sanjay Dutt, said something at a press briefing some time later. He insisted that an accused say several things which never come to light as they are not related to the case. For instance, Nikam said, Kasab had told him that he wanted to have chicken and mutton biryani. The media, always never quite satiated by sensationalism, flashed the "chicken and mutton biryani" part all over. I again remember perceptions changing in a matter of a day. The same people who spoke of a "soft-hearted culprit" thundered, "How dare he ask for chicken and mutton biryani after killing so many innocents?"

While arguing cases, Nikam later told me during a meeting, lawyers say a lot many things about their clients. Only relevant points are picked up by the court. However, lawyers have an additional responsibility while speaking about high-profile cases in front of the media. They must know they are creating perceptions on a national level with their utterances.

"One has not only an ability to perceive the world, but an ability to alter one's perception of it. More simply, one can change things by the manner in which one looks at them," said the American author, Tom Robbins. So, remember, howsoever honest you are in your business, if there is a need to create a perception among your staff, in the society or the nation, you must be clever enough to handle that. Perception is a double-edged weapon. It can hurt your opponent and, at the same time, it can hurt you if you play your cards wrong.

❐

95

Think Success to Succeed

Manjit Singh's family hails from Sahiwal, then Montgomery, a small town now in Pakistan. The family relocated to Patiala during the Partition days in 1947. Like every family, even Manjit's father was worried about the son's future after he got his daughter married off to a bakery owner in Ludhiana.

Manjit's sister insisted that his brother stay put in Ludhiana and apart from doing his graduation, he learns the finer elements of bakery business from her husband. A lot of deliberation later, Manjit reluctantly accepted the move and started helping his brother-in-law at his small bakery-cum-shop in Ludhiana.

While still in college, Singh tried his hand at trading in coal, but failed. By the time he became a final-year graduation student, he realised his love for baking and wanted to be in that business. So he dropped out of academics. Scepticism was rife when he started his own bakery in Ludhiana's Madhopuri locality with a second-hand earthen oven and four sacks of flour in 1985. Can he succeed, people asked. He'd married barely four months ago.

Close to three decades later, Manjit, the man behind the Ludhiana-based Bonn Nutrients, is the largest bread maker in North India. He holds 67% market share in the region, producing nearly 600,000 loaves daily. Apart from a range of breads, Bonn Nutrients makes an assortment of buns, cakes, cookies, rusk and biscuits in its bakeries at Ludhiana and Kapurthala in Punjab, as well as at its franchise and contract manufacturing units in several other states in the north. From just ₹ 65 crore in 2004/05, its turnover today has shot up to ₹ 400 crore. Manjit takes good care of his 3,000 employees.

From the very word go, Manjit knew he had no option but to succeed. He has steered clear of many upheavals in the past. The Punjab insurgency was at its peak through most of the 1980s, and at one point, almost halted Singh's business. Then again, his business almost folded up when his salesman and driver were killed in one of the worst terrorist attacks. In fact, no one was willing to deliver his produce. Manjit soldiered on and somehow got his business back on track.

All along, Manjit proved how to succeed by the sweat of his brow. In the initial months, he used to deliver his products to shopkeepers in nearby towns on his scooter. With time, he realised he had to scale up his speed to compete with rivals. Today, Bonn Nutrients has a full-fledged transport department with 400 vehicles to deliver its products.

"Keep your dreams alive. Understand to achieve anything requires faith and belief in yourself," said the American Olympic champion, Gail Devers. Think sharp. Manjit is no superman. He cannot even boast of distinguished roots. All he had by his side were his determination and driving force that he had no option but to succeed. If you closely observe the lives of successful businessmen, the common thread that binds them is their resolve to make it.

❐

96

Money Alone can't Lead to Failure

He is from a middle-class family of Chandigarh and an Arts graduate from Panjab University, Chandigarh. He started his career with Sun Pharmaceuticals as a medical representative, became the leader in Federation of Medical and Sales Representatives Association of India (Chandigarh chapter) for the betterment of medical representatives and fought for their benefits for almost 18 years.

Realising that he can do better for the larger good of the society, 39-year-old Naginder Kumar, with a meager earning of ₹ 7,900 a month, launched a crusade against the malpractices in the local civic body and decided to contest the civic body election. He participated in and organised various agitations for the welfare of pharmaceutical trade.

Soon, his doughty spirit impressed many political parties in Chandigarh and Jan Manch came forward to help him in his crusade. Naginder, who became a Jan Manch candidate from ward number 8, believes that money alone is not required to be a leader. It needs determination, hard work and loyalty towards voters.

Close on the heels of Naginder, Ranjit Kaur, a resident of colony number 5 also decided to contest the civic body elections with the financial assistance of the residents in her ward. Wife of a vehicle driver, she earns a paltry ₹ 2,000 every month and teaches at the Don Bosco Church at Chandigarh in Sector 24. The monthly income of the couple is not more than ₹ 10,000.

These two examples offer a peek into lives shorn of glamour and devoted to helping fellow residents. The backbone of support of Naginder and Ranjit Kaur are not politicians, but local residents. In fact, for both donations coming in the denominations of ₹ 10 to ₹ 50 add up to quite a bit. In a world where only the rich can 'afford' to contest election, candidates like the fearless twosome have shown that public voice can be heard, or more rightly, can be made to be heard.

Though drinking water, playground and local issues remain the driving forces for the two new leaders, equitable distribution of development in all parts of Chandigarh is also part of their list of priorities. Chandigarh may be one of the most beautiful cities of the country, but Ranjit and Naginder aren't resting till they have made it more, much more beautiful.

"The difference between the impossible and the possible lies in a person's determination," said former American Major League baseball player, Tommy Lasorda. History has proved that money alone cannot become the reason for your failure. There are scores of people who have become successful without money. Ranjit and Naginder did not have money, but wanted to do something for the people. The people backed them. That was their real money.

❒

Don't Forget to Thank Your Company Firewall

Mary was a telephone operator in Le Monde, one of the famous and popular newspapers in Paris. She came to work at 10 am, while the other employees arrive post 11 am. That is how newspapers work globally. During one of my exchange programmes, when I worked there for three months, I saw every employee wishing Mary Good Morning and asking "Anything for me?" thanking her for any answer before they moved to their desk. This was a regular practice at the Le Monde newspaper office.

Many may think 'thank you' is a term that denotes gratitude. Then what does Mary possess to merit it daily? When I asked Mary about this, she requested me to arrive at the office at 9 am the next day. I did. At 9 am sharp, telephone calls started pouring in with callers—some upset, some angry and some others impatient—voicing their opinions. The callers were readers, who either disagreed with the reporters' copy, had an opinion about wrong language, badly printed pages, missing supplement and the quality of the paper and content. Mary answered all the questions with patience and promised each complainant that she would certainly revert with answers or solutions.

At 11 am, when another operator came in, Mary took up all the complaints with departments like editorial, production, circulation and marketing, got the answers from them and made an effort to call up those readers who had called.

Like Mary, there are others in companies who take the first impact of a customer's ire. But how many of us have ever walked up to their desk and said, 'thank you'? Believe me, do it once and see the difference. The communication between your company and your customers would improve further. You will certainly have more satisfied customers around the area you operate.

In the modern world, telephone operators are the interface between customers and the company. If you produce quality products and serve only a few elite customers in the area you operate, then you may have fewer problems. But if you are dealing with a mass product like mobile communication business and you provide bad service or product, then your telephone operator is going to be deluged with complaints. And if your operator fails to give satisfactory replies to unsatisfied customers, the chances are that those customers would forsake your product forever.

"Make it a habit to say people 'thank you', to express your appreciation, sincerely and without the expectation of anything in return. Truly appreciate those around you, and you'll soon find many others around you. Truly appreciate life, and you'll find that you have more of it," said the American writer, Ralph Marston. The point here is every company has a firewall, which protects all employees from the customers' ire, more particularly when we produce a bad product. But it is our job to identify those firewalls and appreciate and thank them. In many companies, the firewalls are our telephone operators!

❒

98

Wanna be Sexy? Be Intelligent First

What do women want from their men? Every survey done globally has the same answer. The man-of-her-dreams must be erudite, cosmopolitan and stunningly well read. From Pandit Nehru to Amitabh Bachchan, popular persons adorn the pages of the Indian history, persons who once were and still are most desired by women, irrespective of age.

In his celebrated TV show *Kaun Banega Crorepati,* superstar Amitabh Bachchan has maintained that common sense is all it takes to achieve success and education in essence must go basic academics, inculcating a sharp understanding of everyday issues that happen around us.

Authors of all hues have always suggested five points for achieving common sense: 1. Don't sleep too much. Enjoy being alive and productive. 2. Sometimes, nobody really cares if you are miserable. So, you might as well be happy. 3. If you cannot solve it, it's not a problem – it is a reality. The most successful of people have gone through such stages in life. 4. Happiness is like a perfume; you cannot pour it on others without getting a few drops on yourself. 5. Lastly, if all good things must come to an end, then do not worry. Even all bad things eventually would end too.

If you imbibe these five principles of life, the development of common sense is inevitable, says Woody Allen, well-known American actor whose talent, not looks, still has women swoon over him, more than Clint Eastwood and Robert Redford. Closer home, look at Amitabh Bachchan. Age notwithstanding, he has managed to make heads turn, from 6 to 60.

For people who live on self pity and mouth one-liners like "I am from a small town", "My school or college is bad" and "My parents are uneducated," I recommend a comedy film of the 1980s called *Back to School* by Rodney Dangerfield. In the film, the protagonist asks his psychiatrist, "Everyone hates me. What am I supposed to do?" The psychiatrist scoofs at him, "Well, everyone hasn't met you yet."

The same analogy applies here. So what if you are from a small town, or your college and school was bad or your parents are not educated? It hardly makes a difference. We are talking about common sense and not academics or lineage. It has often been seen that children from smaller towns and relatively unknown places have more common sense than their counterparts in the metros.

"The true sign of intelligence is not knowledge, but imagination," said German physicist, Albert Einstein. So, the next time you feel like becoming popular among girls, in the society or amidst your peers, the only qualification you need is intelligence, aka common sense. Do you have it in you?

❐

99

Age is but a Number for a Winner

Inspired by a leaf, a Pune-based 20-year-student's design for a self-generating water source powered by the sun and capable of producing 20 litres of drinking water everyday bagged an international design award early in 2011.

Aptly titled 'Leaf', it is 18-feet tall solar powered water condensation unit designed by Anurag Sarda. It won the first place out of entries submitted by top design schools across the world for the 'Time to Care Sustainable Design Award'.

A sizable number of young scientists are working towards creating a waterless toilet for the world. Those who use traditional toilets waste roughly 30% of the total water used in a household—up to 13 litres per flush. A young team of Mexican designers has found a way to eliminate the use of water and turn waste into pathogen-free organic compost through their waterless toilet.

In 2011 itself, at a competition organised by Victorinox Swiss Army, a Swiss company popular for their Army knives, one was introduced to Sarda, a student of MIT Institute of Design (MITID) who was then pursuing an internship in Germany and is working on a prototype model, which he said he would complete in the next two years with sponsorship from Victorinox. Sarda's project was then in an incipient stage and he claimed it could be practically implemented in humid regions in Asia, North America, South America, Africa and Australia. Sarda's enterprise was appreciated because it offered a universal solution and was not confined to toilet alone.

That's about the young brigade. On the other side of the spectrum is Fauja Singh who is 100 and is of Indian origin. He ran a 42-km marathon in Toronto in 2011. He accomplished this amazing feat, becoming the oldest man ever to complete such a distance. He started participating in marathons only after he crossed the 90-mark. He took eight hours to cross the 42-km distance, but nonetheless entered the Guinness Book of World Records with the accomplishment.

Well, what do you have to say about the above-mentioned instances where the young is pitted against the elderly? Clearly, the message is if you decide to achieve something, age is certainly not a criterion. "Age is an issue of mind over matter. If you don't mind, it doesn't matter," said the American author, Mark Twain. Never give an excuse that you are too young or too old. If you have the will, you would eventually be a winner.

❒

100

Experience Real Situations to be Creative

Do you remember the Hero Honda advertisement, where a young man is driving a motorcycle on a suspended bridge between two valleys, even as the wooden sleepers in between them are broken? Yet, he tries to make it to the other side of the valley and the advertisement says at the end of the daring act that everyone has a "Hero" within him, a word that promotes self-confidence as well as the brand.

This ad reminds me of my visit to innumerable narrow wooden plank-suspended bridges held by some iron cables connecting hundreds of mountain villages isolated by ridges and ravines of the Himalayas. Among the 50-odd from Darjeeling district alone, if you recall, one of them in Bijanbari collapsed in 2011, killing 32 people and injuring many. In these places, people have no option but to use these hanging bridges day in and day out.

In 2011, an earthquake led to cracks in several bridges, which were built by the British to connect tea gardens with the main road. But since the formation of the Darjeeling Gorkha Hill Council in the late 1980s, little care has been taken to preserve these connecting bridges, which is the lifeline for people belonging to various panchayats, who use them for their daily grind.

Sometimes we watch films in which the hero takes a horse or an elephant to buy groceries for his house. It's amusing as we never see such a thing happening around us. But there is an orthopedic surgeon, Dr. Himanshu Khara, who takes his horse to shop everyday at Ramnagar in Sabarmati in Ahmedabad. Often people stare in disbelief as Dr. Khara rides past them on his horse to pick up groceries. The doctor has four cars parked next to his home and clinic, but when it comes to small errands, he prefers to take his 'Kajal' (his horse) along. He has a unique perspective of Ahmedabad crazy traffic and he does this '*shahi sawari*' towering over the best of the cars in the city on the crowded roads.

If you want to be creative by bringing reality closer to those who are not exposed to such strange things, then you need to experience them personally before making them a promotional tool. When I happened to meet a creative genius like Piyush Pandey (who made the Fevicol advertisement) in 2011 at the Ad Asia 2011 in New Delhi, he said that some creative writer asked his managing director to send him on a holiday to Shimla for writing a copy for beverage company. The holiday over, he came back with a line called "*thanda matlab* Coca Cola".

"Creativity is just connecting things. When you ask creative people how they did something, they feel a little guilty because they didn't really do it, they just saw something. It seemed obvious to them after a while. That's because they were able to connect experiences they've had and synthesize new things," said the American entrepreneur, Steve Jobs. What he means to say is that unless you experience and absorb the real-life situations, it will be impossible for you to transform a 'story' into a 'creative copy' that could make an impact on the consumers.

❒

Have the 'Madness' to Win

They were not experienced motorsport guys, had no experience in motorsport, except that they were mad about driving. Yet, they made themselves and their town proud when they won the prestigious Raid de Himalaya car rally in 2011.

Motorsport enthusiasts from Nashik, Parwinder Sandhu and Paritosh Kohok finished third at the podium. Both participated in the Raid de Himalaya, the world's highest motorsport battle arena, and finished third in the T2 Gypsy, Extreme categories respectively. The rally finished in seven days. The event attracted participants from all over the country. The route of the rally spread all over Himachal Pradesh and J&K.

"The terrain is very scenic and, at the same time, it gives you unseen challenges at 17,500 ft above sea level, with very narrow roads and, sometimes, no roads, just empty patches strewn with gravel surfaces lined with rocks and black ice," said Parvinder. He has won INRC events many times. Coming back after a gap, Parvinder posed a challenge to himself and proved he could do it once again.

Things were not all that easy for the two as on day one, Parvinder experienced breathing trouble and had to take medication. After this episode, the duo matched the challenge physically and mentally. The two also experienced some very exciting moments like the one at the Zozila Pass, before reaching Srinagar, a failed truck had blocked the road. The route was very rough. The riders started from Shimla and passed through Manali, Leh, Khardungla, Wari La (18,000 ft) to Nubra. The rally ended at Srinagar. A total of 44 cars participated in the extreme event, but only 14 managed to reach the finishing line.

The Nashik duo had to change their shock-absorbers 16 times during the event. It's an endurance test for the participants. On many occasions, the service team does not reach to repair your vehicle, you cannot come out of the car as it's always sub-zero temperatures and windy and you are left at the mercy of the nature and military. One needs to be extremely mad or insane to be part of the event. The 99% of credit goes to perfect calls made by them when calamity struck.

"Champions," said ace pugilist, Muhammad Ali, "aren't made in the gyms. Champions are made from something they have deep inside them – a desire, a dream, a vision." I would add one more – a streak of madness. The two motorists achieved this success because of their excellent co-ordination and team work. But, above all, they had the madness that they had to win. That helped them wade through the extremities and come out with flying colours. Do you possess this 'madness'?